STALAG: U.S.A.

Judith M. Gansberg

Designed by Joy Chu

Manufactured in the United States of America

Library of Congress Cataloging in Publication Data

Gansberg, Judith M.
Stalag, U.S.A.

Bibliography: p.
Includes index.
1. World War, 1939-1945—Prisoners and prisons,
American.   2.   United States. Prisoner of War Special
Projects Division.   3.   Prisoners of war—United States.
4.   Prisoners of war—Germany.   5.   Denazification.
I.   Title.
D805.U5G36 1977   940.54'72'73   76-51407
ISBN 0-690-01223-3

10   9   8   7   6   5   4   3   2   1

To Nana, Papa, and Feche,
the best.

AUTHOR'S NOTE

WHEN THE IDEA of writing a book about prisoners of war held within the United States during World War II was suggested to me, I had no idea that upon investigation I would discover a top-secret program unknown to the American public to this day. However, telling the story of this program—of the Prisoner of War Special Projects Division and the unusual plan to reeducate the 372,000 German prisoners—turned out to be a much longer and more challenging enterprise than I had anticipated. The recently declassified records include hundreds of boxes of material, much of it repetitious. Since I was working alone, it took months to weed things out, only to find that many of the most valuable pieces in the puzzle had somehow been lost during the thirty years the papers hibernated.

Every avenue had to be examined in the hope of finding the missing links. The final product tells the story as accurately and readably as I believe it can be told. It combines the bits and pieces of information collected from as many published and unpublished sources as I could uncover, including quotes from many participants on both sides.

I regret that I did not get much cooperation from the German veterans groups, which seem to prefer to forget the war. But each man I found gave me the name of another, and friends helped through personal contacts in Germany, so the prisoner side is told.

In accordance with my agreement with the Modern Military Branch of the National Archives in Washington, which must protect the privacy of people in its files, I have not used the surnames of prisoners whose stories I took directly from those files. The complete names of prisoners appear only if I have personally questioned them (some were interviewed for me by friends), received letters from them, or if their names have appeared in any public media in connection with their experience as POWs.

I have also chosen not to fully identify any Americans if in my judgment they might be unintentionally injured or receive notoriety because of the circumstances in which they were involved thirty years ago.

The task of writing this book would not have been possible without the help of four men: Maxwell S. McKnight, former deputy director of the POWSPD; Judge Robert L. Kunzig, former executive officer of the POWSPD and former commandant of Fort Kearney; Dr. William G. Moulton, former assistant director of the language program at Forts Getty and Eustis; and Edwin Casady, former instructor at Forts Getty and Eustis. The interviews and material they gave me were invaluable.

I would also like to acknowledge most gratefully the help of the following: Robert F. Richards, Brigadier General S.L.A. Marshall, Lauretta N. (Mrs. Alpheus) Smith, Dr. Walter Hallstein, Curt Vinz, John Hasslacher, Dr. Gustav René Hocke, Rudolf Werner, Sid Richman, Ron D., Josef K., Lori Palomone, Mrs. Howard Mumford Jones, Peter Davison, and my brother, Alan Gansberg. I also want to make special mention of the assistance I received from William Cunliffe and Bernice Lee at the National Archives.

I am especially grateful for the efforts of my friend and translator Kathe Spitze and my mother, Agatha Gansberg, who worked with her, thereby saving me much time and expense.

I should also like to mention that this book would never have come about if Paul R. Wiesenfeld had not come upon the subject some eight years ago. His cursory research and investigation told him a book was in order. Although I learned after months of research that the real story was quite a bit different from the one he had envisioned, I will always be grateful to him for recognizing a good idea and passing it on to me.

Lastly, I would like to acknowledge two special beings. First, dear Bob, who has spent virtually all our married life living this book with me, encouraging me, and acting as a sounding board for so many ideas. And second, my very special cat, Louis, who until his recent untimely death was my constant companion and comfort through the best and worst days of this manuscript. They gave me the support I needed to—for once—finish something I'd started.

J. M. G.
November 1976

CONTENTS

STALAG: U.S.A.

INTRODUCTION

PRISONERS OF WAR and their treatment have been largely ignored by most historians. Except in cases where horrible atrocities were reported, as at Andersonville during the Civil War and on the Bataan Death March in World War II, or, more recently, the inhumanity of the North Vietnamese, war prisoners are usually forgotten after the conflict ends. Yet, the POW is an inevitable problem in modern warfare. This was especially true for the Allied powers in World War II, who discovered that victory meant caring for an unprecedented number of prisoners.

Of the more than 3,000,000 prisoners of war held by the Allies during World War II, approximately 425,000 were in camps within the continental United States. Of that number, nearly 372,000 were German. Their care at the hands of the American Army comprises a unique and little-known tale of very special men and goals.

These German prisoners are special in the history of prisoner-of-war treatment because a singular set of circumstances affected their lives. For one thing, the Geneva Convention Relative to the Treatment of Prisoners of War, the first enforceable treaty for the handling of prisoners, was in effect. In the United States, at least, that meant good food, work, and warm beds for all. This in itself was unusual. But an unexpected phenomenon, from the army's point of view, also occurred: America was facing Nazism on its own shores. Americans had never paid enough attention to the real nature of the enemy to anticipate how difficult it would be to control until it arrived on their front stoop. The single-minded viciousness of this fanatic philosophy and its followers among the prisoners created an inevitable demand for a plan to reeducate the Germans held in the United States in order to draw them away from National Socialism.

The reeducation program, adopted at the urging of Eleanor Roosevelt, was undoubtedly a violation of the spirit of the Geneva Convention's provisions against denationalization. It was a massive multimedia effort to bring about a democratic trend among the prisoners which would not only change their views but could also provide a vanguard for redirecting postwar Germany. This program, above all else, made the captivity of the Germans within the United States a unique experience, for it was the first and only American POW program designed to do more than just hold the men captive.

The numerous wars of the late nineteenth century finally convinced world leaders that there was a need to settle the matter of what one was supposed to do with war prisoners. In response, twenty-six nations agreed to the Hague Convention of 1899, the first agreement of its kind to be ratified by so many powers. In a section on prisoners of war, it outlined the duties of both the captor and the prisoners. Although revised in 1907 to correct earlier deficiencies, the convention's main failing, the section which bound signatories to the agreement only if *all* the belligerents had signed, was not altered. Since Serbia and Montenegro never signed the 1907 treaty, ironically the only treaty binding the United States and Germany as to prisoner treatment during World War I was the antiquated Treaty of Prussia, signed in

1785 as a result of the experiences of Hessian prisoners during the American Revolution.

Fortunately, the total number of military prisoners held in the United States during that war never exceeded 1,346, although nonmilitary internees brought the figure to 5,887. Such a small number of men was no trouble to maintain and a mere microcosm of what was to occur in the next war.

After World War I, the problems of POWs was finally faced honestly by the United States and other countries. Two international agreements, the Geneva Convention Relative to the Treatment of Prisoners of War and the Geneva Red Cross Convention, were signed in 1929. The latter defined the status of captured sick and wounded, medical and sanitary personnel, and chaplains ("protected personnel"). The former, commonly referred to simply as the Geneva Convention, contained ninety-seven articles aimed at improving the lot of prisoners of war. It outlined work, recreation, food, health, and sanitary requirements, certain rights belonging to the prisoners, and all obligations of the captor to the prisoners.

Allegedly to complement international efforts, the U.S. War Department began to make its own plans. In July 1924, Brigadier General S. D. Rochenbach was made acting provost marshal general and ordered to draft plans for a military police corps which would be mustered, on the president's directive, if war broke out. Rochenbach's proposed manual governing the corps, not actually published until 1937, included instructions for maintaining prisoners of war. It gave control to the provost marshal general and his agents and clarified many previously undefined aspects of POW life, such as use of prisoners as labor.

In July 1941, with war on the horizon, President Franklin D. Roosevelt selected Major General Allen Gullion as provost marshal general to deal with expected MP and POW operations. His first prisoners of war were the crews of seized alien ships who were interned in the United States and the approximately 18,500 civilian enemy aliens, mostly Japanese-Americans, whom the Army expected to intern when the inevitable war with Japan began. (Camps were begun before Pearl Harbor for the projected civilian prisoners.)

Later that year, anticipating war, President Roosevelt announced that American shipping would be protected by force if necessary, and the navy informed General Gullion that prisoners could be expected. Under the World War I agreement, which both parties agreed to honor, all prisoners of war became the responsibility of the army under the provost marshal general. Preparing for military prisoners for the first time, the PMG submitted a request to build one internment camp. The first prisoner was captured on December 7, 1941, on a minisubmarine at Pearl Harbor.

Early in 1942, the War Department decided that all prisoners captured by the United States should be transferred stateside. According to Maxwell McKnight, at the time chief of the Administrative Section of the POW Division, Camp Operations Branch, PMGO, this decision was made to alleviate the problem of feeding and housing prisoners in the war zone. "If we kept prisoners in such large numbers, under the Geneva Convention, we would have had to supply them with all kinds of food and medical needs of one kind or another," he explained. "This would have cut down our transportation facilities to support our own troop efforts." But ships returning to the United States, virtually empty, to pick up new troops and supplies could easily carry prisoners.

Very few prisoners were captured by the American Army in 1942 but many were held by the Allies, and in August the British proposed that the United States take 50,000 British-held POWs on one month's notice and an additional 100,000 on three months' notice. Great Britain already held over a quarter of a million prisoners, more than it could conceivably feed and house properly, and because of the urgency of the request, the deputy chief of staff, Lieutenant General Joseph T. McNarney, directed the

Joint Staff Planners (JSP) not to be overly cautious about security and to consider that this was a necessary part of the total war effort.

The JSP, opting for safety, ignored McNarney and recommended that only 50,000 be accepted for internment and that the rest be sent to Canada. They feared that such a large number would create a threat of sabotage to American industry and war production. It was a very unrealistic look at the growing prisoner problem.

But security was a crucial issue. "In those days," remembers Maxwell McKnight, "no one made any provisions for anything other than security, because we assumed the vaunted Afrika Korps was going to be the toughest kind of thing. And there was one experience in World War I. Prisoners escaped. They had blown up something. Jack McCloy [John J. McCloy, assistant secretary of war] was very much involved with working on this because of the 'Black Tom' thing.* We were very conscious of these things from a security standpoint, so our whole concentration was—you build the damnedest and cheapest that you can for security purposes."

The Joint Chiefs of Staff overrode the recommendation of the JSP, calling it impractical, and agreed to accept all the British prisoners in question. Then, in November, the Joint Chiefs agreed to take another 25,000 men held by the British in Kenya. Had all of them arrived on schedule, the United States would have been swamped with over 75,000 prisoners by the end of 1942 and 100,000 more shortly thereafter. Fortunately for the PMG, which had only thirty-six MP escort companies and a few camps prepared, the British delayed. By mid-1943, when the rush began, sufficient guards and beds were available.

Prisoners were first housed in old Civilian Conservation

*German undercover saboteurs were believed responsible for the destruction of the New Jersey Black Tom munitions plant in 1916, resulting in a twenty-two-million-dollar loss.

Corps (CCC) camps or in unused camps built in the Southwest for enemy aliens, but as the program rapidly became larger than the army had anticipated, the War Department realized that these camps could never hold the expected number of prisoners. In a matter of months, internment camps were built to hold 78,218 more men, and construction was begun to accommodate an additional 144,000 if needed. Emergency use of tents was the rule until the men could be properly housed.

Along with the predictable problems of housing and feeding such a large contingent of prisoners, the army discovered it faced other, unexpected problems. The scourge of Nazism was carried over into the American camps. Among the captives there was more fear and distrust of one another because of politics than there was of their captors. This distrust nurtured Nazism more effectively than Hitler himself could have done. Putting several thousand captives together in one camp inevitably created brutal covert battlefields.

Showing uncharacteristic flexibility and realism, and with a determined push from the White House, the War Department recognized both the necessity of finding a solution to this situation and the potential for being the chief long-range beneficiary of its own solution. To accomplish the task, a branch of the Prisoner of War Division of the Provost Marshal General's Office, the Prisoner of War Special Projects Division (POWSPD), was created in 1944.

The small group of talented and dedicated men selected for the POWSPD in just a few weeks' time devised and put into effect a plan to reeducate 372,000 Germans on a crash schedule. By creating one of the most remarkable and most successful training programs ever implemented under the auspices of the military, they virtually deactivated National Socialism in the POW camps. The project remains today a unique experiment in political reprogramming.

◀ Welcome to America

"Now we too had to walk the bitter road behind the barbed wire," wrote Helmut W. the night after his patrol was captured by British troops in North Africa. The May 1943 defeat of the Afrika Korps resulted in the wholesale shipment of prisoners to the United States, and the War Department, although it knew that victory in North Africa would inevitably mean thousands of prisoners of war for the Allies, was almost overwhelmed. Camps were being built all over the country, but the system was not ready for 130,000 POWs by August, to say nothing of the 200,000 more who would be arriving within the following twelve months. The Provost Marshal General's Office began to gear up rapidly.

An inexperienced jailer, the army had not anticipated the endless problems created by the moving of large numbers of prisoners in the midst of battle. Although new regulations in 1943 required "only minimal" paperwork—fingerprints, information tag, personnel record, serial number, and photograph—for each prisoner before sending him to the United States, a plethora of problems arose because of the confusion in a combat zone and poorly coordinated advance planning.

To make matters worse, there was no interbranch cooperation. Intelligence officers often confiscated the soldier's *Soldbuch* (a paper version of the American dog tags) for their intelligence value and ignored the standing order to return them to prisoners for the use of the PMG. Since the *Soldbücher* contained much of the information the processors needed, much time and paperwork could have been saved if they had not been taken.

In addition, no one had thought to consult with the top field brass about POW movements. Thus, the PMG was surprised to learn that the commanding general of the North African Theater of Operations refused to allow POW-processing units near the battlefield. In his opinion, the twenty-eight-man units would occupy space that could be better used for combat troops. So, POWs sat in collecting centers—really no more than large barbed-wire pens—or were shunted around from camp to camp while the army tried to find ways to process them.

According to Helmut W., the first night in his collecting center, things went well. He noted: "The Americans brought water with big water tanks. We still had enough to eat. In the evening tents were built and the poles of the barbed-wire fences had to serve as tent poles."

But life deteriorated rapidly while they waited for the army to organize. Helmut W. wrote:

> During these three days, we were wandering in Camp Mateur from one corner to the other. At the end we were divided in groups of 100 each. The sanitary facilities are dog-gone miserable [*hundsmiserabel*]. A latrine is out of the question. At one end of the camp a place is cleared and they relieve themselves on the ground. Since no one wants to stand in the waste of the other man he takes his place

somewhat farther away and in the end there's an amusing sight. Cone after cone lay there in rows to an approximate width of ten meters. With great pains we later receive a few spades so that we can dig a few ditches. . . . A shovelful of dirt at least makes the whole thing a little more sanitary. . . . There is practically no water for washing. For rations we have stew and cans of hash.

Then, without warning, the hundred-man group to which Helmut W. was assigned was wakened at 3:00 A.M. and transferred to a camp near the port of La Calle, Algeria, where the guards were Free French and cans of meat the only food. Later that same day, they were moved to a British-run camp, Camp Morris, nearer La Calle.

At Morris, the prisoners were issued tents but no tent poles. Since by ten in the morning the sun made any tent too hot to stay in, the missing poles were of lesser concern than the lack of certain other amenities. As Helmut W. wrote: "There were only four water taps for 8,000 men and this meant that you had to stand in line for hours in the burning heat." One meal a day was served—at 3:00 P.M.—consisting of white bread, canned corned beef, canned potatoes, a slice of fruit, a dab of marmalade, tea, and sugar. There were no facilities for heating water.

Camp Morris was so close to a port that the men assumed they would be shipped to England or America and decent accommodations soon. But they were too optimistic. On May 25 they boarded an ancient French freighter, which took them from La Calle to Bône. They were still being routed for processing. Helmut W. wrote: "I am glad, of course, that at least I don't have diarrhea like many of my comrades because on deck there are only four empty cake cans. In these you have to try and rid yourself of your *sächelchen* with greater or lesser ingenuity in a stormy sea!"

From Bône, the prisoners were marched several kilometers

to what Helmut W. called a "real camp." Exhausted from their trip and travel sickness, only their pride in German superiority kept them in step under the burning sun. The English, Helmut noted, confiscated "knives, straight razors, scissors, blankets and shelter-halves." For the first time since their capture, the men had real tents and blankets, but the food remained inadequate.

At last, preparations for evacuation to the United States began. The men received typhoid shots and medical care, the paperwork was done, and interrogations began. On August 5, three months after his capture, Helmut W. finally boarded a ship bound for America.

Three weeks later, he arrived in Norfolk, Virginia. Predictably, the prisoners were first examined for lice, then their clothing was confiscated and they got their first real baths in a long time. Clean clothes were then issued, and they boarded Pullman cars for the trip to their final destination. Helmut W. observed in true German form (many prisoners made the same comment) that "the interpreters are, of course, Jews. To an extent, very worthy representatives of their race."

While hundreds of complaints were filed with the Swiss about the conditions in North Africa, in all fairness not all prisoners had it quite so rough as Helmut W. Conditions in most North African camps were at best Spartan, but the frequent discovery of Italians from French-run camps as stowaways among the Germans on United States-bound vessels attests in some measure to the degree to which American-run camps, even in North Africa, were more humanely managed than those of our Allies.

Men like Richard S., an officer's orderly, fared relatively well. Captured by the British in North Africa, he was "taken to an empty place and searched for weapons, ammunition, compass, maps, etc.," he wrote. "From there we went to Tunis, where two camps were already overcrowded. . . . We had been in camp for eight days when the Tommy came with slips of paper. 'Leave on word of honor.' Thus one hundred men could go bathing every day. Each of the one hundred had a slip of paper saying that he promised not to escape. . . . It got nicer out there with every passing day."

In the shuttle for processing, Richard S. got separated from his officer and was transferred by train to an American camp in Casablanca where, he wrote: "Everything was taken away from us. We were searched and received one blanket each. There were scores of tents and always two men were assigned to each tent. We played soccer and handball, did boxing and other sports . . . we arranged one big and beautiful variety show. Several of our comrades had musical instruments. It was really splendid."

Weeks later, he was transferred to another, less comfortable American camp where the commanding officer punished misbehavior by shutting off the water. But within a few days Richard S. was bound for the United States on a troop transport ship. "Soon we saw the first victims of seasickness," he wrote. "In one way that was rather nice, for we could eat their food rations, thus catching up on what we had missed in Africa."

Once the Italian campaign was well under way, processors were finally allowed to go to the front lines, speeding up their work. But too many men had already been too rapidly loaded onto ships in an effort to get them out of the combat area, with no effort made to coordinate with the PMG's people.

The anticipated surrender of Italy gave authorities the opportunity to reduce the confusion. The assistant provost marshal general, Brigadier General Blackshear M. Bryan, halted the shipment of Italian captives from North Africa in September 1943. But this merely eliminated the problem of establishing separate camps for the Italians; it did not slow prisoner arrivals in the United States. The number of POWs swelled as German prisoners from Sicily, Italy, and from British camps in North Africa replaced Italians on United States-bound ships. Reluctantly, the PMG admitted that the War Department still had no idea how many prisoners the army might ultimately have to intern, although estimates ran as high as 500,000.

After September 1943, Germans arriving in the United States came from every battlefront in Europe. Those captured in Europe were much luckier than those interned in North Africa. The climate was less grueling, and with fewer prisoners to handle at one time, the army could move them out more rapidly. Reinhold Pabel was captured wounded in Italy. In his book *Enemies Are Human*, Pabel describes what happened.

After emergency field surgery was completed, he was quickly transferred to the hospital ship U.S.S. *Solimon*, where he reported that German soldiers aboard were treated in exactly the same manner as Allied servicemen. The wounded were taken to the Fifty-third Hospital Station in Bizerte, Tunisia, a complete, well-staffed medical center. There, the doctors worked with professional detachment and equal efficiency on all patients, with only one exception observed by Pabel: "There is a German POW in our ward who is not very bright and, to make it worse, is only half-conscious most of the time due to the constant pain in his genital region which is a hopeless shambles of torn flesh. Captain X makes a practice of inducing the patient to concede certain atrocities committed against Jews. He would stop in his treatment periodically to let his question sink in. The poor victim would admit anything to get relief from his pain."

After he recovered, Pabel was shipped aboard the *Empress of Scotland* from Casablanca to Norfolk. An educated man who spoke relatively good English, he had read American books and magazines during his hospital stay to prepare himself for the trip. He recalled that many prisoners less adaptable than he seethed with anti-American feelings nurtured in the North African camps, but the coffee and sandwiches served in modern, upholstered train coaches in Norfolk helped many forget these early resentments.

Security worries, lack of finished camps, fear of negative

public reaction (citizens living near Camp Shanks, New York, for instance, complained bitterly when they discovered POWs in the neighborhood), and still imperfect processing made the army reluctant to transport stateside more prisoners than it regarded as absolutely necessary. Finally, in late 1944, the War Department decided it had absorbed its fair share of prisoners and the accompanying headaches, and shipment to the United States was stopped.

But it was only a temporary respite. While debate continued within the War Department, commanding officers in Europe argued that they could not possibly cope with the problems of feeding, housing, and maintaining required security for the growing number of prisoners. POW maintenance was draining badly needed supplies and manpower from combat operations. More important, as it turned out, it hadn't taken long for government officials, congressmen, and agricultural groups to realize that prisoners could be used to relieve the farm labor shortage. They exhorted the War Department to send them more "workers."

Congressional pressure tipped the scales, and the army agreed to admit a limited additional number of POWs. In February and March 1945, 6,000 prisoners arrived at American ports, to be followed by 60,000 more in April and May. The last 3,000 arrived on May 13, 1945, five days after V-E Day. They raised the total number of Axis prisoners in the United States to 425,871. Of these, 371,683 were Germans.

While Reinhold Pabel felt that anti-American feelings among the German prisoners were somewhat eased by the good food and comfortable conditions they found in the United States, such gains were often nullified by the hundreds of cases of missing POW property.

Their Hitlerite education had taught the Germans that Americans were disorganized, undisciplined, and senile—characteristics Germans despised the most. The Property Branch of the Enemy Prisoner of War Information Bureau at Fort

George G. Meade, Maryland, did nothing to dispel that image.

Under the Geneva Convention, a prisoner could keep personal possessions other than potential weapons or cash (to finance escapes), and if any property was taken by the processing authorities, the prisoner signed an inventory slip and obtained a receipt. Unfortunately, the system broke down on many occasions and complaints multiplied. Medical instruments, watches, pens, eyeglasses, cash, cameras, and untold other items were "misplaced." Naturally, the sheer volume of property contributed to the confusion at Fort Meade. But, too often, tags were lost or items added to a GI's "souvenirs," and many possessions were never returned to the rightful owners.

Another cause of prisoner dissatisfaction was an inevitable and unpleasant necessity of war: interrogation.

Helmut W. and Reinhold Pabel both remembered their first encounter with interrogation vividly. According to Helmut W., the British were brutal and ruthless in efforts to get tactical information from his fellow-soldiers in Africa. He wrote: "Men are being taken out of various compounds and sent to Algiers for questioning. The latest trick of the English is now to threaten the men with arms and thrash them with sticks while they were questioned in case they failed to give the desired answer."

Pabel was first interrogated while under anesthetic awaiting field surgery. "Just before they put me on the operating table to fix my wound temporarily some fellow kneeled down beside me," he recalled. "He must have been one of those psychological warfare boys who take advantage of enemy soldiers still affected with the numbness of battle fatigue and ready to spill everything. He asked: 'Do you think Germany can still win the war?' "

Immediate questioning upon capture on the battlefield often took advantage of the wounded, as in Pabel's case, or posed a distinct and obvious threat to frightened men. Years later, a former field intelligence officer readily admitted having shot a German captive in the head to induce his comrades to talk. But that was only a first step. Prisoners were questioned at every stop along the way to the United States, and again in American camps.

Intelligence men were looking for many things. Of course, immediately important tactical information had to be gleaned on the battlefield, but there was much nontactical data that prisoners could reveal at later interviews. Such information might include overall strategy, scientific knowledge, economic or industrial facts, names of spies, or details of the high command. Prisoners who seemed like good candidates as sources of valuable information were flown from the theater of operations to either Forts Hunt and Tracy near Washington, D.C., or Byron Hot Springs in California. Two other camps, Pine Groves Furnace and Fort George G. Meade, were also used as interrogation centers for prisoners who arrived by conventional ship transportation but appeared to be worth extra questioning.

These special intelligence operations were almost blown wide open by foreign correspondent William L. Shirer. Shirer claimed to have hitched a ride on an Air Transport Command plane carrying a group of selected prisoners from Europe to the United States. He erroneously reported that prisoners were taking spaces in planes that were supposed to be used for wounded GIs. Fortunately, before printing his story, the *New York Herald Tribune* consulted with the War Department's Bureau of Public Relations. The paper agreed that under no circumstances should the German government be apprised of such an airborne operation, and it killed the story. Oddly, after a full investigation, the army never found Shirer's name on any arrival list, so it never determined who was responsible for letting him on the special flight.

At the interrogation centers, under constant surveillance through listening devices, the prisoners were questioned by Allied officers. For a time, the United States attempted to infiltrate cooperative Germans into the groups of prisoners waiting to be interrogated. However, this method backfired with unfortunate consequences when a U-boat prisoner, Werner Drechsler, a collaborator with the intelligence branch at Fort Meade, was recognized and hanged as a traitor by fellow prisoners at Camp Papago Park, Arizona, on March 12, 1944.

Intelligence teams traveled from camp to camp to question new arrivals and reinterrogate others. Generally speaking, POWs were loyal to their fatherland and quite naturally resented the intensive grilling each was required to undergo. Often, complaints were relayed by the Swiss legation in Washington to the State Department alleging that groups of prisoners had been held in solitary confinement and threatened with physical harm or torture if information was not given. Some of these reports were false or exaggerated. For instance, upon investigation, a series of complaints from Camps Forrest, Crossville, and Roswall which alleged that intelligence officers offered bribes and used force to get POWs to sign statements proved to be a fabrication by a few ardent Nazis. But many stories of brutality were true.

The War Department acted to reprimand those in intelligence work only in cases where they lied to prisoners about specific terms of the Geneva Convention. They could starve a prisoner into collapse but could not misrepresent that hallowed protector of prisoners. One interrogator, for example, told a German sergeant in a Southern camp that the Geneva Convention did not protect Germans because Germany had left the League of Nations. He had held the sergeant for three days in a hot, airless room with little food or water, but he was reprimanded only for his lie about the convention. In many reported cases where such lies did not occur, cruel treatment was acknowledged but not punished by the army.

The attitude of the intelligence men was: "What do you think happens to our boys in Germany if they do not answer questions?" No official action was ever taken to modify their activities or dissuade them from their code of ethics. And indeed, later testimony showed that German interrogators had often been physically brutal to American prisoners.

One of the major jobs for intelligence men within the camps was locating men who were not Germans but had been serving in the German Army for a variety of reasons. Maxwell McKnight, at the time chief of the Administrative Section of the POW Division, Camp Operations Branch, recalled that one day a camp commander phoned him and complained, "McKnight, you sent me some Germans, but they don't speak any German. I don't know what they speak, but it's not German." They turned out to be Russians.

Dutch, French, Austrians, Czechs, Yugoslavs, Poles, Arabs, Luxembourgers, Swiss, Russians, Hungarians, Rumanians, and even Jews (at least three Jews were among prisoners in the United States) were among the young men impressed by Germany in the conquered areas to relieve her manpower shortages. A large percentage of these men threw down their weapons as soon as they saw an American, but all were captured in German uniform and counted as German prisoners of war.

Of these, the Russians posed a particular problem. Once the Russian Army began liberating German prisoner-of-war camps, they offered to trade American soldiers for the Russians held in America, whom they regarded as traitors because they had worked for the Nazis building the Normandy fortifications. While their transportation was arranged, the Russian prisoners were gathered at Fort Dix. Knowing that death for treason awaited them in Russia, as a group they refused to go and many even committed suicide. The army had to resort to tear gas to force them aboard trains that would take them to San Francisco. Their shipment home was the only way to assure the early return of Americans then with the Russians.

Other non-German prisoners were more fortunate. Once cleared as anti-Nazi, they were allowed to join Allied units in the field. To be cleared, each had to satisfy four requirements: that he was a true citizen of the country he claimed (native-born or with father or both parents from that country even if he had been born elsewhere), that he was impressed into the German Army, that he held political beliefs compatible with those of the United Nations, and that he was physically qualified.

Camp Butner, North Carolina, a five-thousand-man camp, had a special compound which housed between seven hundred and nine hundred non-German anti-Nazis. Almost a dozen nations were represented, with Poles, Czechs, French, and Dutch in the majority. More than five hundred were repatriated to their own national armies. "It was a great day for them," wrote the assistant executive officer, "when they strode through the gates for the last time in British field uniforms with 'Czechoslovakia' or 'Poland' as their shoulder patch and no 'PW'!"

However, a few countries didn't want men back who had served Germany in any capacity, and their consuls in Washington rejected those who passed the test. A group of Luxembourgers wrote directly to the grand duchess imploring her to let them fight for the Allies.

Those who did not satisfy the requirements or were not welcomed by their own governments were to remain with the native Germans and be repatriated to the country whose uniform they wore on capture, in accordance with the Geneva Convention.

But the problem was not that easily solved. The army was besieged by requests from men who, although born in Germany, claimed other nationalities, having lived most of their lives in other countries. When the Germans occupied their areas, they were identified and drafted against their will. Most had wives and children in Holland or Poland for whose freedom they wanted to fight. A further complication was presented by those German-Americans who had been trapped in Germany while visiting relatives or studying in the winter of 1941-42 and had later been forced into the army, all of whom begged to be released from camp and to be allowed to rejoin their families.

These were difficult decisions, and each case had to be studied and evaluated on its own merits. However, in the interests of security the army dictated that a man had to be repatriated to the country of his uniform unless he could establish by the correct responses to the four critical questions that he was a bona fide citizen of a nation other than Germany. Thus, most petitions were denied, even those of the German-Americans, since they were not native-born. The army was also particularly cautious about this group because they made excellent potential spies for Hitler.

In general, intelligence work in the camps did pay off. Authentic non-Germans were located and enlisted in the Allied cause, anti-Nazi Germans were identified for special reeducation projects, and the army even got the answer to the crucial question of whether Germans had defied Hitler by listening to the American "Freedom Station" or the BBC (88 percent of those responding positively had listened to the BBC). But most important was the uncovering of many SS and Gestapo members wanted for specific war crimes but masquerading as Wehrmacht (regular army).

So strong was the fear that these men were concealing their identities in order to organize prisoner disturbances, escapes, sabotage, and to pursue Nazi politics in Allied territory that intelligence work was particularly intense to find them. Once investigation showed that many members of the elite Waffen SS and Allgemeine SS had tattooed a badge of membership in their left armpits—to the untrained eye the marks looked like blood-type indicators—intelligence men at POW camps were required to examine all armpits for the telltale tattoo.

By the combined efforts of British and American intelligence, fourteen of the SS troops responsible for the murder of American prisoners at Malmédy, Belgium, during the Battle of the Bulge in December 1944 were identified and isolated for relocation for war crimes trials.

Coming from Hitler's Germany, the prisoners were not at all sure what to expect in America. Many were filled with curiosity, while others were convinced of the truth of years of Nazi propaganda and misrepresentation. The ardent Nazis firmly believed that New York City had been bombed to ruins. A fake film they'd been shown, produced by Nazi propagandists, had "proved" it.

Lauretta Smith, wife of Colonel Alpheus Smith, commanding officer of the Special Project in Democracy at Fort Eustis, Virginia, remembers chatting one day with members of a work crew from a nearby pro-Nazi camp who had been taken to New York "in order to scotch their belief." "Some of them still believed that the bus trip had been some sort of Hollywood illusion," she said. "They still thought Germany was victorious."

During their cross-country train rides, many prisoners expressed surprise at not seeing any bombed-out areas, while others noted how rich and bountiful the land was. The most common first reaction, however, related to house construction. Richard S. wrote: "I did not see a single house made of stone. Even Russia looked better than that." "The first impression we had," noted Reinhold Pabel, "was the abundance of automobiles everywhere. On the other hand, we discovered a sharp contrast to this obvious wealth in the poor construction and preservation of the numerous frame houses, especially in Kentucky."

Train travel was the fastest, cheapest, and most efficient means of moving large groups of men, and most POW camps had been deliberately located within five miles of a railroad depot. Special precautions were taken to prevent escapes en route, and considering the number of men that had to be moved (ten thousand in twenty-six separate operations in one day in May 1943 alone), transportation went surprisingly smoothly and complaints were minimal.

Of course, as with any large operation, slipups did occur. The president of the American War Dads was once forced out of his drawing room on a train to make room for ill prisoners who could not travel with the group. In another case, prisoners traveling on a passenger train were fed in the dining car, a clear violation of army policy and the Geneva Convention. *Time, The Washington Post*, and other publications made much of such goofs, to the dismay and embarrassment of the War Department.

After their arrival in the United States, Helmut W., Richard S., Reinhold Pabel, and scores of other German prisoners quickly discovered that their life, or as much of it as the army could arrange for them, was going to be quite comfortable. Most problems would be caused by the Nazi agitators among them. But they could not know that when they disembarked at Boston, New York, Norfolk-Newport News-Hampton Roads, or San Francisco. They were concerned about their personal belongings, food, and immediate comforts as they boarded trains for the long trip to their new addresses for the duration.

2 The Camp Scene

DURING HELMUT W.'S FIRST WEEK at Camp Shelby, Mississippi, it was immediately apparent that the American Army was meticulous about following the provisions of the Geneva Convention concerning the physical comfort of the prisoners. Helmut could readily agree with hundreds of his comrades who wrote home praising the conditions of their confinement.

The food was particularly astounding to men who had been eating German Army rations for years. The Americans were merely adhering to convention rules, which required that POWs be fed the same food as the captor's army. But American soldiers normally ate more than Germans. "Here we eat more in a single day than during a whole week at home," Helmut wrote. "At supper you find most certainly chunks up to a pound in weight. . . . I believe I might almost state that many a man has not eaten so well at home. First of all, it is comparatively rich in variety. We have almost every day apricots, apples, plums or pears. Nothing is missing in the diet.

"We have twice a week cake and pastry; more you really can't expect. The bread, which is not missing at a single meal, is in the main white. Now and then there is a sort of dark bread."

Helmut then listed a Sunday menu: "Breakfast: milk, cornflakes (Wheaties), sugar, bread, coffee, marmalade. Lunch: tomato soup, ribs, potatoes, vegetables, pudding, pastry, tea. Supper: cold cuts and vegetable dish, bread, cocoa, one apple."

Food was so good, in fact, that prisoners wrote their families not to send them food in gift packages, begging them to keep the food for use at home, where it was really needed.

At Shelby, German mess sergeants did the cooking and adjusted the menu to fit prisoner tastes—lots of potatoes, for example, and dark bread. The European cooks were so skilled at making army chow tasty that many Americans assigned to Camp Crossville, Tennessee, took their meals at the German or Italian mess halls whenever possible. As one corporal said: "It looks like these foreigners take their cooking more seriously than we do."

Reinhold Pabel agreed that the food was extraordinary. He wrote: "We at first suspected the Yanks wanted to make fun of us. Such a menu: soup, vegetables, meat, milk, fish, grapes, coffee and ice cream! Never before in our military career had we been served a meal like that."

Nothing was ever wasted. Bones were scraped clean of meat, boiled, and the marrow used in other foods. Whenever possible, leftovers were used in soups and stews. Consequently, so little garbage was collected at the German mess hall that the civilian garbage-removal contractor at Camp McAlester, Oklahoma, canceled his contract because he was not collecting enough refuse to pay for transportation.

Helmut W.'s POW camp was located on the grounds of the army base at Camp Shelby, twelve miles from Hattiesburg, Mississippi. Situated on five hundred acres, it was approximately half woodland and half retired farmland.

The POW enclosure, as at all camps, was divided into four compounds: three residential and one for recreation. All were surrounded by the standard double-woven wire fence topped with barbed-wire overhangs. Helmut noted that the wooded terrain created lots of hiding places for would-be escapers, and he wondered who would be the first to try.

Helmut was one of 3,273 Germans housed at Shelby (2,535 noncommissioned officers, 733 privates, and 5 medical officers). The men, who were predominantly from the Afrika Korps, lived in typical 22-man huts, 16 by 48 feet large. Every prisoner had a bunk (with springs and a mattress) in a double-decker wooden bed.

Camps had been deliberately built primarily in the South, for as Maxwell McKnight explained, "it was more economical. Oil was a problem back in those days, too. If you could have the prisoners down South where the winters were milder, you had less of a problem with heat."

But, the army discovered, there were also drawbacks to being only a few miles from the Gulf of Mexico. One, as most of the Mississippians know, is the weather. Helmut and fellow-prisoner Josef K. both spoke of the intense and, to Europeans, unfamiliar humidity in the summer which hampered work and caused great discomfort. Mosquitoes were another regional problem for both captor and prisoner. To combat them, every building had to be screened and insect control, at some expense, diligent on the part of the base sanitation corps. The mosquitoes, though, could be used—and were—as a deterrent against misbehavior in the camps. At Camp Wynne, Arkansas, for example, sixteen prisoners who refused to increase their work load were taken into the woods and forced to strip and stand unprotected for several hours.

But these were minor inconveniences. American POW camps were relatively luxurious places to spend a war. The camps were built to be functionally comfortable, and many Germans—like Helmut—had never lived so well as soldiers. Hot and cold running water, washbasins, washtubs, commodes, showers, and bathtubs were provided in every latrine. Laundry tubs and washboards were also readily available. There were sterile medical infirmaries (Shelby had three), dental facilities, and even hospitals at some camps. Some camps cost up to two million dollars to build (such as Camps Concordia in Kansas and Tonkawa in Oklahoma, which were not attached to existing military bases), and all were administered by up to 70 officers and 750 enlisted men (primarily guard personnel).

Although the prisoners did most of the heavy labor, all administration of the many branches required American staff. While many communities resented having war prisoners based nearby, the local economies did not suffer. In fact, most received a financial boost from the many Americans affiliated with the camps. At Concordia, Kansas, for example, almost all the available rooms in hotels and apartments were leased for camp personnel and their dependents.

Prisoners lived in two kinds of camps planned for the efficient employment of POWs and maximum use of available housing. The preferred life-style was at base camps planned as permanent facilities for the full administration of prisoner needs. Branch camps (at first called side camps) were designed to fill permanent or temporary work needs as additions to the base camps. While they had their own staffs, branch camps were directed by the nearest base camp.

To conserve on building and for security purposes, about three-fifths of the base camps were located on army posts. Many old Civilian Conservation Corps (CCC) and National Youth Administration (NYA) camps were utilized throughout the war, since new camp construction was banned in 1944 when troop movements out of the country began opening space on military posts. Naturally, the New Deal camps were too primitive to suit the standards of the Geneva Convention, so the army had to improve them for prisoner use.

Besides the necessary living areas, all possible needs were covered by the facilities at most camps. There were maintenance shops, chapels, orderly rooms, a dispensary, a laundry, a canteen for POWs and a PX for GIs, mess halls, workshops, recreation buildings, outdoor recreation areas, and even a POW cemetery.

Prisoners had the option of wearing their own uniforms or the prescribed prisoner outfit. POW clothing was dark blue, marked on the front and back of the shirt, front and seat of the pants with a large white "PW" or "PP" (for "protected personnel"—medical officers, chaplains, sanitary personnel, and so on). At Shelby, as in most camps, the prisoners received a wardrobe to suit every occasion. While the clothes may not have been particularly stylish, the men had coordinated raincoats, summer- and winter-weight clothes and underwear, a wool cap, belt, denim work clothes, gloves, and white socks. And ten POW tailors worked daily at Shelby doing alterations.

Shoes posed more of a problem. Many early arrivals among the Germans refused to wear United States Army-issue shoes. A prisoner at Fort Sam Houston, Texas, explained that the rubber heels on American boots could not be clicked like the German ones when one came to attention or saluted. Germans considered it a matter of pride to be able to snap to attention in the way they had been trained. So, prisoners operated their own shoe-repair unit which kept sharp wooden heels on their shoes. Many wore wooden sandals on hot days. They weren't very comfortable, but they certainly could click!

A prisoner's day began early, usually at 5:30 A.M., at reveille, followed by breakfast. After cleaning the barracks (which were always reported to be uniformly spotless), prisoners were sent out on work details either inside the camps or to an outside contractor. The lunch break at noon gave working prisoners an hour to eat and rest. The army allowed prisoners to work six days a week from 7:30 A.M. to 4:30 P.M.

After the evening meal, always eaten in the camp, a prisoner's time was his own. The Geneva Convention required that prisoners be allowed sports equipment, musical instruments, books, and other such materials to boost morale, relieve monotony, and help keep them physically fit. Many service organizations, such as the YMCA War Prisoners Aid, the International Red Cross, and the National Catholic Welfare Council, helped the army keep recreation areas unusually well stocked with equipment.

Soccer was Helmut W.'s favorite sport, he recorded, and he could have played it every night on one of the several teams competing in the Shelby "Olympics." Or, in the indoor recreation area, he could play chess, cards, skat, checkers, or join many of his friends in arts and crafts projects. Not surprisingly, buxom nudes were the most popular subject of prisoner artists, but there were also Impressionist renderings of their recent experiences— drawings of shanty homes seen from trains in the United States, Nazi art, battlefield scenes, and personal subjects. One talented and enterprising prisoner at Camp Alva, Oklahoma, used scrap material to build a miniature replica of an American house he found in a magazine.

At Camp Shelby, one of the favorite pastimes of the men was catching snakes—usually black water moccasins—skinning and treating them. They would then fashion the skins into purses and sell them to the guards. Helmut's friend Josef K. was particularly adept at catching snakes. "One day on my hunt I saw this little snake resting on a tree stump," Josef remembers. "He was different shades of green, and I thought he would make a most attractive purse. So I killed him and brought him back to camp. The guards were shocked when they saw it, but I didn't know ·why. Then someone told me it was a very deadly species. If bitten, I would have died within minutes."

Noticing how involved the men became in art projects and also how highly competitive about nearly everything they were, some camp commanders arranged to put these traits to work to brighten up the camps. At Camp Aliceville, Alabama, prizes were awarded to the compound which had done the best landscaping job. The Germans rose to the challenge, and the contest was a huge success. Not only were the lawns beautifully kept, but there were animals sculpted out of bushes, flower gardens in intricate patterns, trellises, and carefully planned mosaics fashioned from many different flowers.

Camp McAlester, Oklahoma, had a camp-beautification project that resulted in the construction of a detailed, near-perfect miniature German mountain village.

The Germans' natural love of music resulted in the formation of either a glee club or a band, or both, at every camp. Where instruments were more easily available, many had complete orchestras which gave concerts or performed at dances (sans girls) that were held periodically. Introducing POWs to American music later became an important part of the reeducation program.

Soldiers seem to have a talent for picking up stray animals, and German soldiers are no different. Many kept pets at camps. Later, upon repatriation, some fought—unsuccessfully—to take their pets with them. Camp zoos were populous and often attractive additions to the compounds. The zoo at Camp Crowder, Missouri, contained a bird house (with lovebirds, parrots, and quail), guinea pigs, white mice, rabbits, snakes, alligators, monkeys, cats, dogs, two goats, and a pet pig. All surrounded a lovely handmade fountain that flowed every evening.

Probably the evening activity the prisoners most appreciated was the opportunity to continue their education. Germans have never underestimated the power of a good education, and since the Geneva Convention ordered captors to provide "intellectual diversion" for POWs, many took full advantage of the possibilities.

Through the Swiss, the U.S. State Department had arranged with the Reich minister for science, art, and education to provide classes leading to several degrees in Germany. Prisoners could gain high-school-equivalency diplomas, take final exams for professional training schools, take specialized diploma courses, take primary and secondary examinations for appointment as teachers in elementary schools, or take examinations for appointments as teachers in academies.

Exams had to be taken in the presence of a committee approved by the Reich ministry of education. For example, the committee for a final exam in engineering had to include at least two graduate or professional engineers, mathematicians, or physicists to be valid, but prisoners could take all the preparatory courses even if such men were not among the available prisoners or among the Americans. (In many camps in Germany, American soldiers were allowed to study through a similar education arrangement with colleges in the United States. According to the Red Cross, former U.S. Attorney General Nicholas Katzenbach, for one example, received much of his education while a prisoner in Germany.)

Schools were started at most camps, with prisoners acting as teachers. Many had been teachers or professors before the war or had enough expertise in a field to teach it. American colleges often helped by renting, lending, or donating books to the camp libraries, and those which offered correspondence courses allowed POWs to subscribe provided they could pay for the lessons. (Their work coupons were converted by the army into cash.) Reinhold Pabel took a Persian-language correspondence class from the University of Chicago.

These camp "universities," as they were called, achieved an enrollment worthy of any American college. Many camps offered more than two hundred different classes in an incredibly varied number of subjects. In Italian camps, where there was a high illiteracy rate, prisoners responded to the education program by learning the three R's.

At Camp Shelby's base camp, Helmut W. had seventeen choices, including German, English I, English II, English III, Middle English, French I, French II, Latin, a commercial course, bookkeeping, mathematics, biology, arithmetic, auto mechanics, shorthand, and bookbinding. The branch camps offered world literature, English, world history, bookkeeping, shorthand, German, and anatomy. If he'd been at Camp Florence, Arizona, Helmut could have mastered Hebrew.

In connection with the schools, camps developed large libraries. At Shelby the library was divided into two sections. One held 2,479 "German entertainment books"; the other, 2,824 study and teaching books. The size of the library varied depending on the size of the camp, the effort made to obtain books, and the number of books available.

Through radio, newspapers, magazines, and in many other ways, prisoners were able to keep in close touch with the outside world. Prisoners could write one letter and one postcard per week to friends and family abroad or to blood relatives within the United States. (General officers were allowed five letters and five postcards a month.) "Blood relatives," however, did not include mothers-in-law, and in several cases the neglected women wrote repeatedly to their congressmen about this rule. The prisoners objected, too, but with less fervor. The length of each outgoing letter was restricted to twenty-four lines of writing, but unlimited letters and packages could be received, subject to censorship.

The army allowed brothers or fathers and sons to be based at the same camp (as long as the prisoners used their own money credit to pay for any transportation and guard costs required to bring the family members together).

The prisoners made full use of other services offered to keep them happy. Proxy marriages arranged through the Swiss legation were unusually popular. Helmut recalled that two such weddings were celebrated at Camp Shelby on November 28, 1943, and he wrote at length about the festivities.

The mess hall was decorated for the occasion, and "on every table there were white tablecloths which usually only officers used," he wrote. "At the other end of the hall they have put up a German war flag and in front of it the bridal table."

The gala began at 4:00 P.M., with even the camp commander, his adjutant, and three press representatives joining in. The celebration was elaborately planned. "First our chorus sings a suitable song," recorded Helmut, "and after that a man recites a poem. Subsequently Oberfeldwebel Stigelmeier is making a little speech. Even the Colonel can't help congratulating the bridegrooms."

Before dinner, the *Rosenkavalier* waltz was played, and then the feast began. "One could factually speak of a wedding banquet," Helmut wrote. "There was nothing missing but the wine. In a magnanimous manner, the Americans have put at the disposal of the two newlywedded husbands ¼ liter wine each." Later, one of the bridegrooms used his canteen coupons to purchase a case of beer for the wedding guests.

In the evening, "In order to provide for Max at least some substitute for his missing wife," Helmut remembered, "we dressed a broom accordingly and placed this scarecrow into his bed. This did not quite suit Max so we could do nothing else but hang up the apparatus so the sentry too might get something out of it during his night inspection."

With or without religious fervor—this being frowned upon by the Nazis—Christmas was a special time. And in American POW camps, the celebrations were festive. The German government transferred 1,440,000 francs from a Swiss account to the Swiss legation in 1943 for Christmas gifts "from the Führer" to POWs in the United States. The money was used to try to provide traditional German gifts for all the men.

"The mess hall was beautifully decorated with green branches; the tables were covered with gifts," wrote Richard S. at Camp Maxey, Texas. "Everybody got a *Stollen* [a loaf-shaped cake] as well as fifty German cigarettes and one package of tobacco. . . . At the end of the hall there was a big Christmas tree with candles and a picture of our Führer and above it we had a German war flag. . . . We sang Christmas carols and then came the best part—Santa Claus heavily laden with gifts." Richard added: "None of us had thought it would be as pleasant and nice as that. . . ."

As was to be expected, senior officers among the prisoners led a life even more comfortable than that of the enlisted men. There were several separate compounds for Axis generals and other senior officers. Each lived in a private bungalow and had an orderly whom he paid the going rate of eighty cents a day. Officers, not required to work under the Geneva Convention, received monthly allowances of twenty to forty dollars, depending on their rank.

The existence of canteens set up for their own use was a surprising luxury to the prisoners, particularly since many of the personal items for sale had not been available in Germany for years. Shelby, in fact, had seven canteens, one in each of the three living compounds and one at each of four branch camps. Although prisoners were not allowed cash (so they couldn't bankroll escapes), they were issued coupons with a dollar value corresponding to the hours they had worked. Prices at canteens ranged from five cents for candy bars, soft drinks, and cigars to thirty-five cents for shaving cream and eighty cents for pipes.

Most prisoners found it impossible to write their families about how easily they could buy things that were only memories at home. Willie V. told an intelligence officer that he would never mention in a letter how readily he could get chocolate, candy, cigarettes, and toilet articles in America, or that he was now eating better than he had even in peacetime Germany. He was afraid that the "American authorities will mimeograph my note and drop it among the German lines with the notation: 'Come on over to us—see how we treat prisoners.' "

Beer was offered in most canteens, at ten cents per bottle, though some COs banned its sale after cases of drunkenness or hangovers had disturbed camp orderliness. Hard liquor was on the *verboten* list at all times. But there are always ways to get around the rules. Josef K. and others at Camp Shelby arranged for an American employee of the pulpwood mill at which they worked to buy them whiskey, which they smuggled back into camp in the tins provided for their lunchtime coffee. At Camp

Stewart, Georgia, American personnel were caught selling liquor to prisoners who had collected a few dollars from pants pockets while working in the camp laundry.

The canteens, with or without beer, were big moneymakers. Although many items were sold at cost, some, like beer and soft drinks, returned a 33.5 percent profit. At Camp Shelby alone, the profits from the POW canteens were $9,308.61 up to February 1945. The money was added to the prisoner fund at the camp and, in place of War Department funds, was used for renting and purchasing sports equipment, movies, music, books, and candy for the 1945 Christmas party which was held after the war had ended.

The War Department made money on another prisoner program, too: the work program. POW employment had begun modestly. Prisoners worked on army posts in non-war-related jobs like watch repairing, gardening, or waiting on table in the officers' mess. But by the time Helmut arrived in the late summer of 1943, critical manpower shortages had begun to develop in both agriculture and industry.

The army decided POWs would make excellent replacement workers as long as their employers did not let them compete with civilian labor or hire them only because they were cheaper than civilians.

While Helmut and Josef received only eighty cents a day for their work in lumbermills, the contractors paid the U.S. Treasury for the labor at the going accepted wage. Since the prisoners' share was decided by agreement with the German government and wages in Germany were lower, the United States was paying the prisoners far less than it received from contractors. It was obvious from the start that profits could be expected, and indeed, in 1944 alone the U.S. government made a profit of $100 million from prisoner labor. Much of the money was used to pay for feeding and housing prisoners and for the materials needed for the reeducation program. So, POWs were basically self-supporting.

The War Department also realized an estimated saving of more than $80 million from work the prisoners did on military posts. For example, a detail assigned to lumber salvage saved Fort Devens, Massachusetts, $385,000 in an eight-month period. Without the POW labor, the army would have had to spend that amount on new material.

During the war, prisoners performed a total of 19,567,719 man-days of work on army posts and 10,181,275 man-days of work for contract employers. More than half of this was on farms. They did every kind of work. In the South they picked cotton, cut sugarcane, harvested tobacco and peanuts, cut pulpwood, and worked in fertilizer plants. In the West they harvested sugar beets and every type of grain. In the North and East they worked in the lumber industry, picked and canned fruits and vegetables.

At Camp Shelby, prisoners worked in pulpwood operations, harvested gum rosin for turpentine, harvested cotton, corn, pecans, tung nuts, and performed all other kinds of farm labor. They also worked in the post exchange and the canteen. The officers' mess alone utilized an average of 1,092 man-days of prisoner labor monthly.

Josef K. traveled from Camp Shelby daily to work in a pulpwood mill in Picayune, Mississippi, owned by a friendly man who offered to help Josef and his family immigrate to the United States after the war. He put Josef in charge of a group of black mill hands. "Realizing," Josef said, "that America was the greatest land of opportunity," he decided to accept the offer. But the more he worked with the blacks and saw how they were treated, the more his decision wavered. One day, to get him to do more work, the boss slapped a man who had lost his leg working in the mill. "At that moment I was so upset I decided this was not the land for me," Josef recalled. Even though he was a product of Nazi Germany, he realized he could not "live in a place where the Negro population was treated so poorly."

Outside Camp McAlester, Oklahoma, the availability of prisoner labor helped many farmers and ranchers to stay in business during the war years. Gene W., a rancher near McAlester, had lost all his ranch hands to better-paying war-plant jobs. He and his wife could never have operated their three-thousand-acre spread without the forty prisoners they contracted for. "They've been our salvation," he recorded in 1943.

Although many of the men had never before worked farm machinery, they were quick to learn baling, oat threshing, and other chores. The only difficulty Gene remembered was "in having to show them, instead of telling them what to do," because of the language barrier.

The prisoners were never shy about making friends with the people around them while they worked. American actor Ron D. remembers German POWs from McAlester working for the rodeo near his home. His mother used to take him there often, and one day, while they were watching rehearsals, several of the Germans cleaning up the stands came over to them. "I was a very blond, Aryan-looking child, so the Germans were drawn to me," Ron recalls. "I guess I reminded them of their own children, and they couldn't get over how German I looked. They were very friendly and spoke some English. We talked and joked with them for some time, until the rodeo manager ordered them back to work."

Problems did arise occasionally. Prisoners on work details were supposed to receive adequate lunches to take with them. At Camp Benjamin Harrison, Indiana, a sample worker's lunch included salami, ham, rolls, hard-boiled eggs, apples, coffee, canned milk, and Italian bread. But the Provost Marshal General's Office discovered that every once in a while prisoners were underfed. Cotton grower and Congressman William M. Whittington of Mississippi called the PMG in a fury after examining the lunches served to the prisoners he hired from Camp Greenwood. Each got only "one boiled egg, six slices of bread (rye or some darned mixture), about a good tablespoon of some kind of grease mixture (similar to some kind of gravy) between two slices of bread, and a canteen of coffee." Whittington complained that one could not get a good day's work out of men who were not fed enough to do hard labor in the hot sun.

The PMG discovered that the quartermaster at Memphis was bitter toward Germans and had decided they could eat "sowbelly and fish for bologna." Farmers had been supplementing the meals—which was not part of their contracts. General Bryan, the assistant PMG, personally corrected the problem.

To get a contract, a contractor had to use at least fifteen prisoners because the army could not spare guards for smaller numbers of men. Safety regulations and all government rules for prisoners of war were strictly adhered to, which meant mining and other jobs considered dangerous were forbidden. Nor were prisoners permitted to do war-related work under the Geneva Convention, but in 1944 the army redefined the jobs that were "war-related," and POWs were, in fact, allowed to work at the Chemical Warfare Center at Edgewood Arsenal, Maryland, and on jeep assembly lines. When the Swiss objected, the army claimed the specific chemical projects and the vehicles the prisoners were working on were safe and would not be used in combat.

Predictably, there was some initial opposition to the prisoners from organized labor. Despite regulations that unions always had to be consulted in fields where labor agreements were in effect, and be given the opportunity to recruit civilians before POWs were hired, organized labor impeded the prisoner work programs whenever it could. It was particularly successful at blocking use of prisoner workers at the Chicago stockyards, where fewer than a hundred were ever employed.

War department meetings with the American Federation of Labor Building Trades Department at long last resulted in an agreement to ban prisoner labor from construction crews if civilians were available. In return, the A. F. of L. informed its members that if workmen were not available in sufficient numbers to complete a job, a contractor could use prisoner labor until civilians could be found.

By April 26, 1945, 91.3 percent of the non-officer prisoners held in the United States were working. There was still a large unfulfilled demand, but by V-E Day, May 8, prisoner labor was needed to rebuild Allied countries in Europe and it was impossible for the War Department to bring over any more. In late 1945, however, the secretary of agriculture and some congressmen argued so successfully that POW labor was essential for the harvest that President Harry S. Truman announced a sixty-day delay in repatriation for those men contracted out in the sugar-beet, cotton, and pulpwood industries. Helmut W. and Josef K. would have to wait another two months to go home. But Truman refused to alter the plan to have all prisoners out of the country by July 1, 1946. So, in May 1946, three years after his capture, Helmut was replaced in the pulpwood mill by a returning veteran and quickly checked out for the trip back to Germany.

Throughout the war years, the army steadfastly defended its treatment of war prisoners against charges of "coddling" or "pampering" by the press and Congress, firmly believing that the POW's good life, filtering back to Germany in letters, was a major contributor to the large number of Germans surrendering. Brigadier General Blackshear M. Bryan, the assistant provost marshal general, testified before the House Committee on Military Affairs investigating the issue that "interrogations of German prisoners of war who surrendered voluntarily indicate that an overwhelming majority of them expected good treatment."

Safe-conduct passes containing a promise of good treatment and signed by General Dwight D. Eisenhower himself were dropped by air. "Considerable numbers of German soldiers came to our lines bearing the safe-conduct passes in their hands," General Bryan told Congress. He explained: "Eighty-six percent of those captured shortly after D-Day, eighty-two percent of those captured during August 1944 and over ninety percent of those captured in October 1944 had accepted the fact that the United States treated prisoners in accordance with the Geneva Convention, despite German efforts to make them believe otherwise."

Hitler is alleged to have been so outraged by the large

number of surrenders that he ordered the murder of all captured Allied airmen in February 1945. He wanted to make German soldiers afraid of American reprisals for mistreatment of Allied prisoners. "If I make it clear that I show no consideration for prisoners," Hitler proclaimed, "but that I treat enemy prisoners without any consideration for their rights, regardless of reprisals, then quite a few [Germans] will think twice before they desert." Admiral Karl Dönitz eventually convinced the Führer that this was not the best way to resolve the problem, and the murders were not carried out.

The War Department believed that any deviation from the standards set by the Geneva Convention would mean sure reprisals against Americans held in Germany. Department officials knew that American and British POWs were getting better care in Germany than prisoners from other countries because of the treatment given to American- and British-held German POWs. But after stories of the horrible conditions in some German camps reached America, Congress launched a full investigation of comparative treatment. Twenty-five camps in the United States were compared with German camps studied by the Swiss.

The House Committee on Military Affairs concluded that the German government was endeavoring to meet the standards of the Geneva Convention. The differences in care, the committee agreed, which caused the furor among the American press and public, stemmed from the anti-American attitudes of a few camp commanders, a less liberal interpretation of certain provisions of the convention—particularly as to food—and the growing military and food-shortage crises in Germany. What Americans did not understand was that food, especially meat, was scarce in Germany. Only the influential ate well. Later, occupation officers would be surprised to discover how many SS officers suffered from malnutrition. In 1944 the Wehrmacht and the German public were not too much better off than the POWs. The food was simply not there to serve to them.

The "coddling" question was a popular issue in the press by mid-1944. Editorial writers in national magazines and most newspapers began questioning the humane American treatment of Nazis. Repeated stories of poor conditions in German camps periodically rekindled the controversy. About the same time Americans liberated from the Orb camp spoke of being given broth made of dehydrated grasses, the Second Service Command reported that POWs were now being served "only" hearts, liver, and kidney as meats.

Frequent reports of fabulous meals and living quarters, mostly exaggerated, brought the PMG on the congressional carpet more than once. One congressman told the wire services that he had seen menus "typical of the Waldorf-Astoria" and Germans getting two free packs of cigarettes a day at Camp Papago Park. Reporters discovered the charges to be "a myth" in March 1945. Julian Hartt, reporting for the International News Service, declared the strong charges against the army "patently untrue" after his own tour of that and other camps.

As a result of the many military and political investigations and those of the press, the truth finally came out—the prisoners were actually receiving care and rations as required by the Geneva Convention, but little more. Suddenly the press flip-flopped. The cry became a more tempered argument for the "American way of doing things." As an editorial in *Collier's* put it in August 1944: "We ought to be humane and generous in this matter because we are Americans and because we believe as a nation in decency, humanity, humaneness and a break for the underdog, which war prisoners surely are." Revenge or retaliation, *Collier's* and others agreed, was not in the true American spirit.

Toward the end of their internment, prisoners noticed a few changes in their food and in their freedom to honor the German Army way. They were stripped of all rank on V-E Day, May 8, 1945. By January 4, 1946, most camps had been cleared of all the external trappings of the Third Reich—flags, ceremonies, salutes.

The men themselves were more annoyed with changes in the menu than the end of Nazism, which the reeducation program had already begun to discredit. The army had removed much from the POW diet, claiming that heightened demand for meat and protein foods among the soldiers of an occupation army required the change. The prisoners believed it was either a punishment for the losers or the typical response of a winner now that there was no longer any fear of reprisals against prisoners of the Nazis. John Hasslacher, a former prisoner at Camp Trinidad, Colorado, remembered that food was not ideal, but there was enough meat and variety until V-E Day. "The moment the war was over," he recalled, "the daily rations consisted of: Porridge with a bit of milk in the mornings, pea soup with lettuce salad and a slice of soft bread (of little nutritious value) at noon and in the evening. I believe coffee or tea was also served." All the prisoners began to lose weight. Several older prisoners at Trinidad died of causes their comrades believed were directly related to the new diet.

The post-V-E Day regulations allowed beef to be served only twice a month (it was eliminated completely by May 1946). Margarine replaced butter at all times. Eggs became a rarity. More vegetables were added to replace the rationed items, and dried prunes became the only available fruit. Cayenne pepper was always used instead of black pepper because of alleged shortages.

Nonworking POWs began to volunteer for work more and more after V-E Day. In the Eighth Service Command, for example, more than two thousand noncommissioned officers voluntarily applied for work in December 1945. The reason for this sudden urge to work, quite possibly, was less a motivation to keep busy or help out than a response to post-V-E Day rules prohibiting noncoms who were not "cooperating fully" with the army from purchasing beer, candy, soft drinks, or cigarettes in the canteens.

Unlike the obvious external alterations, many changes were being brought about under the surface subtly and gradually. The growing political situation in the camps, particularly that of Nazis terrorizing other prisoners, had become a major impetus for an army program to ease the tension.

3 The Cause

WHILE AMERICAN TROOPS fought in North Africa, Europe, and the Pacific, a battlefield was developing at home—in the prisoner-of-war camps spread out in forty-four of the forty-eight states.

As the number of prisoners increased, so did the number of battles within the camps. Caused by Nazi terror tactics, the covert war forced a confrontation. The United States recognized a mammoth obligation to try to alter the course of history: we had to devise programs that could end the tyranny for all time.

Although once born the program grew rapidly, it had a slow, painful delivery complicated by American ignorance of the problem and poor early camp management.

The POW camps were a "dumping ground" for U.S. field-grade officers who were found unsatisfactory for combat and for retired reserve officers. "We were pretty much dredging the bottom of the barrel. We had all kinds of kooks and wacky people," attests Maxwell McKnight. Men were selected in haphazard fashion, often merely because they knew a few words of German. They were sent in to face the fires of National Socialism, the most fanatic of all contemporary political philosophies, yet they were untrained, unskilled, and unaware of what to do to smother the flames.

In many cases no one was responsible for decisions. When POW camps were located on military bases, the commanding officer reported to the post commanding officer. This often led to uncomfortable relations between the two men, a lot of buck-passing, fuzziness of authority, and delegation of responsibility to subordinates. The problem was finally tackled by the Provost Marshal General's Office in 1945 in order to facilitate reeducation.

It was in late 1944 that orientation programs for camp officers were finally begun and related pamphlets distributed. For many Germans it was too late. Many had already died or been seriously injured by careless Americans or at the hands of the Nazis.

The COs did not know what might be required of a guard, and no screening procedures had ever been considered by the army until tragedies began to happen. For example, several mentally ill GIs, rejected for other military assignments, ended up at POW camps.

One private had been court-martialed twice and had never seen combat duty. Still, there was a war on, and the army could ill afford to waste manpower, so he was assigned to a POW branch camp of Fort Douglas, Utah. On the night of July 9, 1945, he had a few beers and wandered back to the camp where German POWs working on the beet harvest were asleep in their tents. Silently he loaded a .30-caliber machine gun, pressed the trigger, and methodically began strafing the forty-three tents. Eight men were killed and twenty wounded. In the investigation that followed, the private confessed he hated Germans and wanted to kill them. The army had never thought to question whether a man had strong feelings about the enemy before placing him on prisoner duty.

One month later, a similar incident occurred at Camp Ashby, Virginia. A guard fired seven rounds into the POW compound because he did not like Germans and wanted to "get" one. Mercifully, this time no one was injured.

There were also many cases of prisoners being killed or wounded in accidents caused by irresponsible or careless guards. In July 1943, there were four such "accidents" at Camp Trinidad, Colorado. One man died. Officers with an ax to grind found other ways to express their revenge against the POWs. At Camp McAlester, Oklahoma, a lieutenant regularly beat the prisoners with a stick because he resented the stiff-arm salute they used. (The German salute was not banned until V-E Day.) After several instances of severe injury, the army reluctantly admitted the officer was "unsuited" for POW duty.

The problems with personnel did not affect camp security, however. There were only 2,803 escapes, and as of October 1946 only 24 POWs were still at large, all of them German. By May 1953, only 4 were still unaccounted for. In addition, 56 prisoners were shot attempting to escape, 34 of whom died. At a press conference held on February 13, 1945, the provost marshal general, Major General Archer L. Lerch, favorably compared the escape rate of .45 percent to that of federal penitentiaries, where the rate was .44 percent.

J. Edgar Hoover, head of the Federal Bureau of Investigation, warned the public in an article in *American* magazine that every escaped prisoner-at-large "trained as he is in the technique of destruction, is a danger to our internal security, our war production, and the lives and safety of our citizens." Hoover had no possible evidence for this statement. The worst crime committed by any escaped prisoner was car theft. There were no incidents of sabotage by escaped prisoners.*

---

*By order of the secretary of war in 1942, FBI and other civilian agents could investigate prisoners only on matters involving violations of American laws but not concerning any internment matters.

Prisoners escaped for many reasons. The most common were boredom, depression, and "Dear John" letters which created an urgency to return home. Some "attempted escapes" really involved overreaction by guards when prisoners got too near the fence in the course of an athletic event or other activity.

Despite a congressional act of April 30, 1945, which created stiff penalties for helping POWs escape, in a few cases Americans were directly involved. In one instance, two Germans broke out of a camp in Michigan with the aid of a guard who went AWOL with them. The three were stopped trying to enter Mexico. The GI's court-martial was rocked by the revelation that eight other soldiers and five WACs had also been in on the escape. In May 1946, two Chicagoans were convicted for helping a cousin to escape from Camp Grant, Illinois.

More often, however, escaping prisoners simply hailed rides or got food and work from unsuspecting local citizens. The people were not pro-German, just ignorant. A man driving down a highway in Illinois would never guess the hitchhiker he picked up to be a German prisoner. Millions of Americans have foreign accents, so a POW was rarely even suspected.

Women were particularly vulnerable at a time when so many young men were unavailable on the home front. Often a prisoner would escape, spend a few hours or a few days with a woman, and then voluntarily return to camp. If he spoke adequate English, a POW could easily woo a woman who was unaware of his prisoner status. Such was the case of Warner S., who escaped from Camp Pomona Ord. Depot, California, and was found twenty-five days later living with a woman on the outskirts of Pomona.

But most prisoners escaped without help. All the usual methods were attempted—cutting wire fences, jumping from trains. Eight men even tried jumping off the H.M.S. *Queen Mary* and swimming for it.

The most spectacular escape in terms of numbers occurred on Christmas Eve 1944 at Camp Papago Park, Arizona. While other prisoners staged a noisy diversionary demonstration, twenty-five men led by Captain Jurgen Wattenberg, former executive officer of the pocket battleship *Graf Spee*, tunneled out into the desert.*

All the Papago Park *Kriegsmarinen* were recaptured, including Captain Wattenberg, who was picked up in Phoenix a month later. In his February 1945 press conference, Provost Marshal General Lerch mocked Wattenberg: "The only thing he could do was get to Phoenix, Arizona, which is about six miles from Papago Park. . . . He was supposed to be a superman and the best he could do was get to Phoenix."

Reinhold Pabel detailed his own 1945 escape in his book *Enemies Are Human*. Unable to tolerate either confinement or the Nazis in his camp any longer, Pabel decided to escape. Luckily for him, he had saved the aforementioned article by J. Edgar Hoover. Using it as a guide to mistakes *not* to make, Pabel slipped out of the Washington, Illinois, branch camp of Camp Ellis. He followed the FBI director's advice and lost himself in a big city, Chicago, taking the name Phil Brick. After holding several jobs, including one at the *Chicago Tribune*, Pabel was running a secondhand bookstore and was married, with one child and another on the way, when apprehended by the FBI in March 1953. With the help of Senator Paul Douglas and other Americans, Pabel returned to Germany and was allowed to reenter the United States with nonquota immigrant status.

Another escaped POW was caught in 1953, when his mother-in-law spotted his picture in the post office and turned him in.

There were very few instances in which escaped prisoners actually left the geographical boundaries of the United States. Besides the Mexican case, two escapees from Camp Scottsbluff, Nebraska, managed to get to Canada, where they worked for a

---

*Wattenberg had escaped captivity in Argentina in 1939, only to be recaptured as a U-boat captain in 1941.

while. They were caught in Philadelphia trying to board a ship bound for Europe.

One man actually did make it back to Europe. After his escape from a camp in Oklahoma, he thumbed his way to Baltimore and got a job on a Lisbon-bound freighter. From there he made his way across Europe until recaptured after V-E Day within miles of the German border. Usually, though, prisoners who escaped in the United States suddenly became aware of how big a country it is. Many surrendered when they realized how far away a port or international boundary was.

The serious results of inadequate training and administration were most evident in the Nazi reigns of terror within the camps themselves. The army suffered from an early inability to detect and deal with the fanaticism of Nazi elements within each camp.

"We'd brought in this vaunted Afrika Korps, and the whole Nazi control was moved right into our backyard," remembers Maxwell McKnight. "And believe me, I could see that as I visited the camps. Who could best get a work detail cracking? The Nazi noncoms. And the guys would go out swinging in the morning to work details singing the 'Horst Wessel' song. They were going to show these Americans on the camp posts! The efficiency in the laundry at every camp, post, and station where we had prisoners increased a hundred and fifty percent. And beautiful work! I mean, shirts came out clean! And at night they'd go back, and, of course, they'd go into the camps singing the Nazi songs."

Although the ardent Nazis were a minority among the prisoners, they managed to conduct the same rule of terror, through violence and threats, that their leaders did in Germany. Few had the courage to challenge them.

The army estimated that perhaps 10 to 15 percent of the enlisted men in the German Army were hard-core Nazis. A higher percentage probably existed among the noncommissioned officers and junior officers. These numbers were duplicated in the prisoner-of-war camps. Members of the Afrika Korps were particularly fanatic.

The Nazis were able to flourish because too many camps were run like Camp Concordia, Kansas. During 1943, the nearly four thousand prisoners at Concordia were subjected to oppressive control by the Nazis among them while the first commanding officer, a retired regular-army colonel, backed away from taking responsible action even with his own subordinates.

A "country club" atmosphere existed on the American side of the wire, and, according to Raimund B., "once you went inside the barbed-wire it was Nazi Germany again." The prisoners ran their own affairs. Work did not get done. Two anti-Nazis were forced to commit suicide. (Men were pressured into suicide when Nazis claimed they had ways of ordering punishment of families at home unless the men agreed to self-punishment for their "treason.") Numerous others were beaten for "unpatriotic behavior."

The Nazi organization was similar to the Gestapo. Courses were organized in military and ideological training; personal conversations were monitored to detect dissenters. Many prisoners kept a club by their bed for protection and used buckets at night rather than dare the dark trip to the latrine.

The Nazis controlled the camp university curriculum as well. They monopolized camp media, censored reading and film material, quashed any sign of anti-Hitlerism, and threatened violence to those who dared protest. Anti-Nazis who died under mysterious circumstances (alleged accidents or suicides) were denied services by German chaplains or German mourners. One was even buried in a segregated grave where he would not "contaminate" his purer Hitlerian ex-comrades.

The army finally awakened to the crisis at Concordia when a brawl between two drunken American officers resulted in the accidental shooting of the CO's wife in December 1943. The colonel was transferred out, along with much of the staff, and a new CO assigned.

The situation then began to change at Concordia. Unfortunately, it didn't change that quickly at many camps.

Once they got settled in, the Nazis moved swiftly to gain control in most camps. Typical of their activities was the experience of Ludwig W., an anti-Nazi prisoner at Camp Mexia, Texas. Ludwig W. described some of the Nazi maneuvers to his captors months later:

> The first camp spokesman was designated by General von Varst. He also regulated the form of camp organization and the conduct of officers. . . .
>
> A short time after the generals had been moved to a special camp the underground struggle for the political leadership of the camp began. . . .
>
> I would guess the Nazis and the anti-Nazis were about even in number. The Nazis organized themselves very quickly, and first tried to shake the position of the camp spokesman, who was not completely in favor of their efforts, by parading placards with inscriptions hostile to America, such as "who are you fighting for" and "Jewish Hirelings."
>
> The camp spokesman at that time, Major S., hereupon took over the responsibility of keeping this schism from coming to the notice of the camp commandant, that is that demonstrations be carried on in the *common* interest only.

But no one really had the courage to challenge Nazi wrath too long. There had been too many years of painful experience in Germany. "After the Nazis had put up placards with the inscription 'He who is not against the Americans will be punished' the spokesman backed out. The camp changed its spokesman four or five times until the struggle for political leadership swayed definitely in favor of the Nazis."

Ludwig W. reported what happened next:

> The Nazis, through their leader, Lieutenant K. [a Nazi Party official], then demanded and got recognition and enforce-

ment powers of the following regulations: the right to censor the newspaper, the right to control use of the radio, the right to control political indoctrination, the right to control use of free time, the right to control criticism of the motion pictures, the right to hold a "court of honor" and a party court and the right to censor mail.

When prominent Nazis were transferred out they appointed their successors so that the activity of the party organization was carried on without interruption.

Ludwig W. reported that control was tight and followed the familiar Nazi practice for maintaining absolute power. Punishments were meted out to violators. He recalled:

Every American film was adversely criticized before its presentation. One officer remarked that he was capable of forming his own opinion of a movie. The Nazi placed him under arrest in quarters. A party court proceeding was held. He was told the affair would have a sequel in Germany after the war.

Another officer admitted the Allies had won considerable success. He was brought before a court of honor and punished by arrest in quarters.

Nazis strictly forbade work for officers and NCOs. After going to work two officers were expelled from the camp brotherhood by the court of honor.

Those who attended religious services were labelled "Reactionaries." Once the cross was stripped from the barracks which served as a church.

Studies were supervised by the Nazis . . . science [and] history were given in a form colored by the Nazi doctrine. Once a week there is a Nazi lecture. Every two weeks there are readings from *Mein Kampf*.

Ludwig W. explained that Germans were conditioned after years of Hitler not to resist for fear of their lives, but he believed that in the event of the fall of Germany or of the Nazi regime "the pent-up bitterness of the anti-Nazis will explode into acts of violence against the terror of the Nazis in the camps." This, however, did not happen.

Further explanation of the pattern of Nazi control among the POWs was added by Karl P. from Camp Trinidad, Colorado, who told American authorities that

> in the Nazi camps the first test put to the *Lagerführer* by the "group that sets the tone" . . . is that of his attitude towards Americans. This decides whether they will tolerate him or not.
>
> If he should as much as even try to collaborate with the American camp commander—even for the benefit of the prisoners—he will either immediately be marked as a "traitor, deserter and spy," or he will immediately be "assisted" by a reliable Nazi adjutant.
>
> . . . The adjutant is the most influential and the most obviously prominent party official. Among other acts of the adjutant at Trinidad was the order that two officers be excluded from the camp community and that the others "not only beat them, but beat them to death."

Usually the terror was directed by "courts of honor," kangaroo courts organized in each camp by the Nazi elements. "Holy Ghost," the German Army term for severe beating, became a commonplace occurrence on the order of these courts. Many soldiers were driven to suicide to save themselves or loved ones from pain. Germans were so indoctrinated into believing the SS to be practically omnipotent that they thought almost any threat made in America could somehow be carried out in Germany. They were convinced that messages were passed in the bandages of repatriated crippled and sick prisoners, by radio, and perhaps through cooperative Americans to the SS and Gestapo in Germany.

Typical of how the Nazis terrorized anyone they felt was not a believer is the story of Gottfried S. at Camp Breckinridge, Kentucky. Gottfried's father, an anti-Nazi college professor, had died at the Dachau concentration camp after the SS had systematically crushed both his legs. His mother had been declared insane and gassed to death in an asylum. Gottfried himself had been a member of the Social Democratic Party, Hitler's chief opposition before he took control.

For weeks the POW fanatics toyed with Gottfried. They tore up his letters from home before he could read them, smashed his wristwatch, mutilated his wife's picture, spit on or put ground glass and dirt in his food. They beat him every time he tried to shower, so he began showering at 4:00 A.M., before the water was heated, hoping his antagonists would not awaken. He lost twenty pounds, became extremely nervous and shaky, but was afraid to ask the Americans for help, fearing that the Nazis might do more in revenge.

After many weeks of this harassment, the Nazi leader approached Gottfried and told him that his "traitorous" behavior had been communicated to the SS in the Reich. In reprisal, the leader alleged, his wife had been taken to Dachau. There was only one way to save her, he warned, as he handed Gottfried a half-full beer bottle and walked out.

Gottfried committed suicide by slashing his wrists with a piece of glass that same night.

At least five murders and countless suicides were positively traced to clandestine Nazi organizations in the camps. There were dozens of other suicides and severe beatings in which Nazi pressure and threats were suspected as the cause.

Fourteen Germans were eventually sentenced to death by American courts-martial and hanged for committing murders in POW camps. Five men (Walter Beyer, Berthold Seidel, Hans Demme, Willi Scholz, and Hans Schomer) were hanged for the murder of a POW, Johannes Kunze, at Camp Gruber, Oklahoma; Erich Gauss and Rudolf Straub were convicted and hanged for

the willful strangulation of Horst Günther at Branch Camp
Aiken, South Carolina; and seven men (Helmut Fischer, Fritz
Franke, Günther Kuelsen, Heinrich Ludwig, Bernhard Reyak,
Otto Stengel, and Rolf Wizuy) were executed for the beating and
hanging of Werner Drechsler at Papago Park, Arizona.* One
prisoner, Edgar Menscher, who beat POW Hans Geller to death
at Camp Chaffee, Arkansas, had his sentence commuted by
President Truman.

All the accused argued to the last that they were merely
carrying out their duty because the victim in each case was a
"traitor."

Leon Jaworski, the U.S. special prosecutor during the
Watergate investigation in 1974, was one of the judge advocate
general's investigators for the Camp Chaffee murder. In his book
After Fifteen Years, he told of the diary of one ardent Nazi
suspected of collaborating in the murder: "On those occasions
when a prisoner-of-war was beaten by others for failure to adhere
to the Nazi line, Ludwig recorded it in his diary with gloating
satisfaction. . . . He detailed the victim's suffering and agony
with glee, and was quite pleased that such an excellent job was
being done of disciplining and punishing 'defectors.' In fact, the
more blood and gore, the better he seemed to like it."

Jaworski recalled, too, how well the Nazis could conceal
the truth. Other prisoners refused to talk for fear of their own
lives. One of the reasons the Chaffee murderer had his sentence
commuted, in fact, was that prosecutors felt he was not alone
in the crime, but they could not get anyone to name his co-
horts.

In April 1944, Nazis at Camp McCoy, Wisconsin, used the
cover of a near riot to beat several anti-Nazis. When the victims

*The Drechsler death was due, at least in part, to army negligence. Drechsler had
been an intelligence plant among naval POWs at Fort George G. Meade. The navy had
warned the army never to send him to a camp where he might be spotted. But army
regulations said navy men had to be interned with navy men. At Papago Park were the
very sailors he had spied on. He died less than twenty hours after his arrival at the camp.

testified against their assailants, who were later sent to the federal penitentiary at Fort Leavenworth, Kansas, it was regarded as a major victory by the Judge Advocate General's Office. While the men themselves were transferred to other camps for their own safety, they fully believed that reprisals would fall upon their families at home.

No one was immune from Nazi menacing. Even fanatic members of the German medical corps kept a tight grasp on the sick whenever they could. At Glennan General Hospital, Oklahoma, prisoners established a Nazi hierarchy from the senior camp spokesman on down to the lowest levels. German doctors working in the POW wards exercised great political power right under American noses and with their unknowing blessing. The patients dared not disobey their doctors. Anyone who complained to an American physician was labeled "queer" or psychotic by the Nazi doctors and risked being locked up in the psychiatric ward. The senior spokesman also had American consent to speak for the enlisted men, who had tried to select a more moderate man as their representative. Only the Nazi view was heard.

At several camps German medics refused to aid injured or sick prisoners whose politics they questioned unless they chanted "Heil Hitler" and saluted beforehand.

The fanatics were extremely well organized, almost as if they had trained for internment in advance, and managed to do more than just dominate their own camps. The stellar work of the Nazi minority, by far, was the sabotaging of the POW postal unit at Camp Hearne, Texas.

Hearne was the central post office in the Southwest, processing approximately seven million pieces of mail between March 1944 and February 1945. Two to three hundred noncommissioned officers, part of a group of "noncooperatives" transferred to Hearne for segregation, distributed the letters and packages. This particular group of men had refused to take farm jobs but were eager for postal positions. The army complied, only too happy to have them working.

All mail was handled by prisoners under the supervision of American officers. Directory service was provided along with the mail. This meant that the postal workers, a significant number of whom wore skull-design rings indicating SS membership, had access to the names of other prisoners and their camp assignments.

They tampered with already censored mail, adding messages of their own to friends in other camps. They also passed uncensored mail from camp to camp illegally. Prisoners would leave old envelopes already bearing the censor's stamp with friends when transferred to another camp. They could then contact each other by marking the envelopes "Not at [name of the camp]" and remailing them with new messages inside. Many who were prisoners at other camps deliberately used Hearne as a return address. That way, they could write to a known person at Hearne, addressing him at another camp, and when the letter returned to Hearne, a friend in the postal unit would see that the addressee got it. (Only blood relatives could legally send letters between camps.)

The Hearne Nazis compiled a blacklist of men who had been Social Democrats or members of other pre-1934 opposition groups. Their access to the directory and mastery of ways to get around mail regulations made it easy for them to locate suspected anti-Nazis and to pass the word to other Nazis in the same camps with the "traitors" so they could be properly threatened.

The postal sabotage was the only Nazi tactic to achieve any success over their captors. Most others failed. The Nazis particularly tried, for example, to thwart the POW work program, which was extremely important to the war effort because it freed American men and women for arms production and other defense-related work and helped to feed all Americans. Attempts to halt work had little effect. Camp after camp reported Nazi-inspired strikes. Some strikes actually lasted a few days, but most ended once the strikers got sufficiently hungry after a diet of bread and water. Only one resulted in any kind of violence. At Camp Chaffee, Arkansas, an overzealous American officer ordered his men to bayonet two striking Nazis who had agitated all the POWs into refusing to do work "beneath their honor" for several days. The bayoneting (in the seat of the pants) spurred the men back to work after some face-saving negotiations.

Overall, strikes and minor sabotage within the camps—small fires or damage to military vehicles—had little or no effect on the productivity of the prisoner-workers. And while it was the Nazi noncoms whose supervision on work crews determined the degree of discipline in most cases, many Americans gradually picked up tricks of keeping workers in line, German-style.

A captain at Camp Wheeler, Georgia, learned to stand rigidly erect in the presence of prisoners, and, holding his gloves in his right hand, flop them back and forth, occasionally slapping them on his left palm. When asked by another American why he did such a seemingly "foppish" thing, he replied, "This sort of glove handling has been a custom of the true Junkers, the caste that produces most German generals, for more than a hundred years. To the ordinary German soldier, it has become an unquestioned symbol of authority. He recognizes and responds to it from force of habit, even when it's used by officers of the army that captured him."

Prisoners did succeed in holding Nazi celebrations, mainly because most American commanders did not know what they were. At Camp Trinidad, Colorado, and many other camps, Nazis held *Morgenfeier* celebrations, rituals similar to religious ceremonies, in honor of Alfred Rosenberg, the leading Nazi Party theoretician. Secret parties were held on Hitler's birthday and other Nazi holidays even after the official American ban on such fetes began being enforced.

Fanatic Nazis formed hara-kiri clubs or suicide clubs in many camps. Their plan was, on Germany's collapse, to attempt mass escapes and kill as many Americans as possible before themselves being killed or committing suicide. To gain members for the club, at Camp Alva, Oklahoma, Nazi leaders spread the lie that the

POWs would be sent to Russia for punishment after the war. By V-E Day, however, the Nazi cliques had been too well dispersed by reeducation efforts for the plans of the clubs to materialize.

Perhaps the best-publicized individual "Nazi" incident of the war was also the most trivial. On February 7, 1945, prisoners from Papago Park were being driven by truck through nearby Chandler, Arizona, to work in the cotton fields. The *Kriegsmarinen* hung a homemade banner (a black swastika on a red background) from the rear of the truck. The town marshal spotted it. He pursued the truck and stopped it near Lemon's Country Store. The offending banner was removed, but unhappily it had already been seen by most of the local citizenry. Suddenly every Chandlerite had a story to tell about some misdemeanor committed by a POW—such as whistling at women or making obscene gestures from moving trucks—for the benefit of the national press.

The story made rather overstated headlines in papers across the country. The *Atlanta Constitution* quoted a War Department spokesman's comment on the affair: "Citizens should remember that young men between 20 and 30 years of age are the same world over. Our soldiers, imprisoned by the Germans, also try to annoy their captors. It's a game they play."

Trucks carrying prisoners were then ordered to bypass Chandler.

It took American authorities many months to realize that *German* and *Nazi* were not synonymous. The largest vote the Nazi party received in a free German election was 37 percent in July 1932, when it won 230 seats. In the last free election in November of that same year, the party actually lost 34 seats. There were many, many dedicated anti-Nazis, some of whom were every bit as militant in their beliefs as the Nazis were in theirs.

Americans were equally surprised to discover that many Afrika Korps prisoners were not Afrika Korps at all. When Hitler established the 999th Probationary Division, he had filled it with men considered "dangerous to the Reich." There were cut-throats, murderers, thieves, rapists, and so on. But a large number were members of the anti-Nazi intelligentsia—newspaper publishers and editors, writers, Democratic Socialist Party members, artists, professors—who had first been sent to prison or concentration camps, then drafted into the 999th when added manpower was needed.

Imagine yourself a camp commander, suggests Maxwell McKnight, "nervous as he is with all these new prisoners, and suddenly he finds a whole group, some of whom speak fluent English, and they want to fight for the United States. The air force people sent intelligence officers to interview these prisoners. They got a wealth of information as to factories and all kinds of things."

But it took a long time before the army located and then decided what to do about these men. Only the most ardent had been sufficiently courageous (or sufficiently frightened of what Nazis might do to them in the camps) to speak up voluntarily upon arrival. They were housed in segregation compounds at several camps. The rest, unconvinced that the Americans could protect them, kept silent, like Gottfried S., and endured.

When the toll of dead and injured began to mount, the army at long last began to comprehend that something was amiss. To the PMG, the problem appeared at first to be the anti-Nazis; after all, they were regularly involved in fights and other "trouble." But someone started listening to their stories and realized that they were the victims, not the perpetrators. The authorities decided that these anti-Nazis should be singled out, preferably through intelligence examinations.

Unfortunately, the exams normally took place at tables set so near each other that the prisoners could hear each other's responses. No anti-Nazi could risk having a Nazi sympathizer hear him declare a loyalty other than to the party. To make matters worse, the questioners weren't allowed to ask a man's political affiliation directly—the German had to volunteer the information. Many did not know that the first move was up to them or that the interrogators would be responsive. A few of the most ardent spoke out; the rest remained silent. Many writers who touched on this question in the press in 1943-44 considered this American lack of foresight to be the single most important reason for beatings and murders in the camps. James H. Powers wrote in *The Atlantic Monthly* that our examination procedures would surely indicate to the Germans that "it doesn't matter much what a prisoner's political views are" to the Americans. Consequently, the army was not finding and protecting its potential allies in the POW camps.

Although the army was very slow to act, it is clear that someone in the War Department had recognized a need to break the Nazi grip in the camps as early as March 1943. That month a proposal was referred to General Frederick Osborn through General George C. Marshall requesting that a plan be drafted by which "prisoners of war might be exposed to the facts of American history, the workings of a democracy and the contributions made to America by peoples of all national origins."

General Osborn passed the job on to Brigadier General S. L. A. Marshall. Marshall recalls the sequence of events vividly:

I was distant from Washington on a very critical operation. So I knew nothing about it until, returning to the Pentagon on a Saturday night, I was told by Osborn that the plan had to be on [George C.] Marshall's desk by 0800 Monday morning. At that point, I blew my top, went to Washington to take on a snootful, just to clear my head. Sunday I wrote the plan. But it was a stop-gap fraud. I knew it was good enough to bank the fires until I could determine what the problem was all about.

Then I got Edward Davison into uniform and also called in Col. Dave Paige, . . . at the time a Military Government Officer. Paige was sent to England and Maj. Davison and I went to Canada to see what was happening to the German PWs. We found the top Nazis and Fascists playing top dog and virtually running the camps. . . .

Then I wrote the *real* plan and substituted it for the dummied-up job. It called for screening the prisoners at once, separating the bad eggs from the amenable ones, ignoring the former and starting education courses for the latter with emphasis on democratic theory and practice. . . .

That plan became pigeonholed in the PMG's office for about one year.

The plan was considered "inadvisable" by the provost marshal general, Major General Allen Gullion. On June 24, 1943, it was deferred.

Gradually, as the camp situation worsened, some of the plan was put into effect merely as a stopgap measure. The army found it had to screen prisoners and separate out the most ardent Nazis. Anti-Nazis who requested segregation were also separated in order to save them from Nazi corporal punishment. Camps Alva (Oklahoma), Pima (Arizona), and Huntsville (Texas) became dumping grounds for "incorrigible" Nazis, just as Fort Devens (Massachusetts) and Camp Campbell (Kentucky) took on an anti-Nazi identity. Gradually, the worst agitators were slowly weeded out of other camps and sent to Alva or separate "segregation" compounds within each camp. As a result, camps began to function a bit more evenly. Prisoners were no longer regularly beaten up if they read *The New York Times* or listened to American radio news programs.

This necessity to separate German from German was at first difficult for the army to comprehend. "We never anticipated segregating despite our experience in the Deep South," recalls Maxwell McKnight. To the War Department, this was quite an earthshaking concept. "We never had a theory of segregating Nazis from anti-Nazis. We could do it on the basis of color, but on the basis of ideology? This never occurred to us."

Despite the changes and the strong censorship exercised on news emanating from the camps, the stories of Nazi atrocities, murders, and forced suicides began to leak to the press.

General S. L. A. Marshall recalls that several months after he wrote his plan, "columnists like Raymond Clapper and Dorothy Thompson began to attack the government and military for defaulting. They pointed out that storm troopers and bully boys were riding herd on all the others; in effect, domineering the camps. The criticism shook the White House."

Miss Thompson and Dorothy Bromley of the *New York Herald Tribune* took the problem directly to Eleanor Roosevelt in late 1943 or early 1944.

Maxwell McKnight, who was then chief of the Administrative Section of Prisoner of War Camp Operations, returned from lunch one day to discover that the White House operator had been trying to reach him. Minutes later, the phone rang and a voice on the other end said, "I'm Mrs. Roosevelt's social secretary. Mrs. Roosevelt would like you for dinner tonight."

Nervous as they were about being in the White House, the McKnights were enjoying their meal with the First Lady and other Roosevelt family members when "suddenly, in the middle of dinner, I guess we'd just about finished the entrée, she turned to me and said, 'Major McKnight, I'm so glad you're here tonight,'" he recalls. "'I've been hearing the most horrible stories from Dorothy Thompson and Dorothy Bromley and others about all the killings that are going on in our camps with these Nazi prisoners. I was told that you would be able to tell me whether there was truth to these stories.'"

McKnight was taken aback by the question. He remembers: "So I wondered what the heck I should tell her. Here's the commander-in-chief's wife, what do you tell her? So I fudged. Well, I told her so much but not the whole truth. After all, I was only a major."

Mrs. Roosevelt must have recognized his predicament and decided the wiser move would be to allow him to speak with his superiors about their conversation. Dinner continued in a normal fashion until the time for good-byes. "As we left and said good-night, she said, 'Major McKnight, we must meet again. I'd like to dig into this. I think it's very important.' "

The next morning, McKnight went straight to Assistant Provost Marshal General Bryan's office. He wanted to know how much information he could give out. Bryan, who had been privy to General Marshall's original plan months before, told him to tell all. McKnight relates what happened: "A couple of days later, I got a call from Malvina Thompson. She invited me to have tea with Mrs. Roosevelt. We—Mrs. Roosevelt, Malvina Thompson, and I—had tea on the South Portico of the White House. I told her the whole story then. She said, 'I've got to talk to Franklin. Right in our backyard, to have these Nazis moved in and controlling the whole thought process! What do you think this does to us?' "

Mrs. Roosevelt did speak to the president. He, in turn, spoke to the secretaries of war and state and several generals. In March 1944, heavy correspondence between Secretary of War Henry Stimson and Secretary of State Edward Stettinius resulted in the revival of General Marshall's plan by the new provost marshal general, Major General Archer L. Lerch.

According to General Marshall: "The PMG dusted off the plan and said something like 'We anticipated the problem all along.' " He added: "By then Paige was Chief of Psychological Warfare Operations in the ETO and I was pathfinding for the Historical Division in the Central Pacific. . . . So the duty fell to Ted Davison who was third down the line, the best man for it in any case."

Colonel Edward Davison, British by birth, was a poet, teacher, and lecturer. He had served on the faculties of the universities of Colorado and Miami before the war and after the war was to become dean of Hunter College's School of General Studies. Davison, with the able assistance of Maxwell McKnight and an international staff of college professors, lawyers, and scholars, was to plan and administer an extremely creditable program. Davison himself was multihonored for his work, including being awarded the Legion of Merit by the U.S. government.

On March 30, 1944, Stettinius and Stimson agreed to start a reorientation program for POWs. Both men felt strongly that there should be no publicity of the project whatsoever and that it should be top secret, at least until V-E Day, for several reasons. For one thing, the War Department feared a counterprogram by Germans on Allied prisoners, teaching them the "glories" of National Socialism. For another, the prisoners read American newspapers and would surely learn of the plan and become resistant to it if it were made public. The State Department, for its part, wanted to avoid a confrontation with the protecting powers over whether the program violated the provisions against denationalization in the Geneva Convention, a certainty if word of the project got out.

The overall objectives of the reorientation program were laid out on August 23. According to a War Department memo, these were: "to give the prisoners of war the facts, objectively presented but so selected and assembled as to correct misinformation and prejudices." These directions were general enough to allow Davison's people much operating room.

Literature, films, newspapers, music, art, and education courses would be used to introduce the POWs to the power and resources of the Allies, in particular America and its democracy. Thus, it was hoped, they would be convinced of the impracticality and viciousness of Nazism. The long-range aim was to form a nucleus of adherents to a new German ideology and the advocacy of a democratic system in Germany.

Mindful that forced anti-Nazi propaganda would be a violation of the Geneva Convention and much too obvious to be effective, the planners decided to fit the program into the rather vague limitations of Article XVII of the convention, which stated: "so far as possible, belligerents shall encourage intellectual diversions and sports organized by the prisoners." By selecting the media used in the Intellectual Diversion Program, as the reeducation program was officially labeled, so as to arouse enough curiosity in the American way on the part of the prisoners so they would ask to learn more, the army hoped to create the means for reeducation.

4 The "Factory"

"THE SPECIAL PROJECTS DIVISION must have been one of the strangest units in the War Office," Robert Richards, a former student and colleague of Davison at the University of Colorado and an air corps communications officer, recalls fondly. "Most of the officers were graduates of the better colleges. They were intellectuals, as was Davison, their director. Therefore, there was an unusual 'esprit' in the department—great friendship."

Through whatever means, Davison and McKnight had managed to put together one of the most remarkable staffs ever assembled when they formed the Prisoners of War Special Projects Division (POWSPD) in the fall of 1944. Davison began by recruiting a German novelist who had fled Hitler, Walter Schoenstedt, as interpreter and adviser on dealing with Nazis, and Robert L. Kunzig, a lawyer and instructor at General Osborn's Information and Education School at Washington and Lee University, where American officers were taught how to prevent unwanted American-German fraternization in Italy (a big problem during the Italian campaign). The eminent Harvard professor Howard Mumford Jones was invited aboard as a planner and teacher. A short time later, Richards joined them.

They were among the first of a group which described themselves in a self-styled spoof:

> A paratrooper, Captain G., was procured just in case it became necessary to drop someone into a compound. A Walt Disney scenario writer came to interpret America in terms of Mickey Mouse. There were others: a Jesuit priest who spent his spare time doing research on Powers models, and who—if he were writing this—would be able to pull off a good pun about reach-search; a Philadelphia lawyer who could push a camel through the eye of a needle if he thought he could sell it on the other side; a child prodigy of the American Poetry Society who was over forty; a former German Rittmeister who could cook up a completed staff study to his own satisfaction in less than ten minutes; and a mystery author who could keep you guessing past the end of any story. In addition, the Division procured a Kostelanetz violinist, a neo-cubic artist, and two or three good-looking Second Lieutenants. Long was the hair that flowed over the desks of the Special Projects Division.

Davison had collected a group of leaders and educators who would make any university proud. They and the special faculty being assembled were tapped for a variety of reasons. Many were personal friends of his. Others knew or were known to Dr. Henry Lee Smith, Jr., the language and dialect expert who is well remembered for his radio series in the thirties, or to Howard Mumford Jones, who handpicked many of the teachers. Dr. William G. Moulton was selected because of previous teaching work with military training programs and fluency in the German language. However recruited, the POWSPD staff, working out of 50 Broadway in New York City, was a unique group.

The most important arm of the Special Projects Division was

to become the "Factory," a special camp where, following the recommendation of the Marshall outline, "selected POWs could be detained and assigned work for assisting in the re-education program." A former CCC camp in Van Etten, New York, with a capacity of 150 men, was chosen as the first home for the special project, which opened October 31, 1944. Five months later, the Factory was transferred to Fort Philip Kearney, Rhode Island, where it remained for the duration.

The camp, a former coast artillery post for harbor defense on Narragansett Bay, became the heart of POW reeducation activity. To assure its success, Captain Robert L. Kunzig left 50 Broadway on V-E Day, May 8, 1945, to become its commanding officer.

Eighty-five anti-Nazi prisoners with skills that could be used for the program were brought to the Factory. Fear of Nazi reprisals made them worried about their safety after the war, so steps were taken to assure their anonymity. Their mailing address was Fort Niagara, New York, an ordinary anti-Nazi POW camp. The editorial address of *Der Ruf* ("The Call"), the newspaper they published for national POW distribution, was listed at a post office box in New York City. The average prisoner could not learn of Kearney's existence.

The prisoners and American supervisors for the SPD, all of whom were cultured, educated men with the same purpose, immediately hit it off as friends and co-workers. All speak, even today, of the "Kearney Spirit"—the comradeship, mutual respect, and cooperation at the Factory.

There was never an escape attempt, because the Germans were there to do a job they felt strongly about. Kunzig recalls that he did worry occasionally that someone might try to escape in the small boat he kept on the bay, but no one ever did. There was just one incident. A few days before his scheduled return to Germany in early 1946, a POW ran off with an American girl. The pair were captured in their room at the Sherry-Netherland Hotel in New York City. It was the only blemish in the entire life of the Factory. Kunzig recalls with amusement: "Poor fellow, he just couldn't wait."

Because of their special assignment and carefully verified backgrounds, the Kearney prisoners enjoyed more freedom than POWs usually did. There were no armed guards or guard towers, and the prisoners would go by ferry to Jamestown in army trucks to pick up supplies. On the ferries they would socialize with the other passengers—people who had no idea they were talking to German prisoners of war. "I know this was true at Kearney," explains Kunzig, "because I sent them."

Worried about what public reaction would be if the true nature of the camp was discovered, Kunzig decided to take Rhode Island's governor, J. Howard McGrath, into his confidence. McGrath kept silent and did a great deal to help the project. Notes Kunzig: "He would help us with all kinds of problems. In other words, we were keeping in contact with the chief officer of the state in which we were physically situated who knew that we did not have police or guards."

As part of this freedom, Kunzig ran the camp in a relaxed, less military atmosphere. His description: "We had almost no problems at Kearney. Once in a while we'd have to sort of jack them up and make sure they kept their beds neat—try to keep it very military and correct. We had inspections, but at the same time there were no real pressures. They could write, work. They had other duties—shoe shining, garbage collecting—but their main work was writing *Der Ruf*.

"The great writers would consistently keep dirty beds. We were always worried about inspection. We had to insist that they make their beds.

"You couldn't follow any rules, they weren't meant for anything like this. If the rule said, 'Thou shalt not wear brown stockings,' and these guys had brown stockings, you broke the rule. The whole program couldn't stop while you got them socks!"

Some problems did occur occasionally with army officers who visited the camp and found the relaxation of military discipline "horrible." Kunzig says: "Then you'd have the problem of people who had loved ones or relatives who had been killed and had a very understandable bitter hatred for Germans. And you could understand these people thinking that any special treatment for prisoners was horrible."

Kunzig remembers that the most exciting and impressive part of the Factory was its personnel—both American and German. "There were some very able people," he reports. "There was Karl Kuntze, who was one of the editors, and a retired publisher in Munich—and still a dear friend of mine—by the name of Curt Vinz. He and a group of others put together a very high-level newspaper.

"There were many others, including Howard Mumford Jones, and T. V. Smith, one of the greatest and most inspiring people. Colonel Smith had been a congressman from Illinois and a professor at the University of Chicago. He was a prolific writer, a fascinating speaker. The students worshiped the guy. We all became great friends."

The prisoners, like the faculty, were chosen by recommendation. Camp commanders were asked for names of particularly able anti-Nazis. The prisoners themselves were an excellent source. Many knew of colleagues who had been captured, and the division could easily find them if they were in the United States. Walter Schoenstedt, one of Davison's leading advisers, and prisoners cleared for the Factory would review lists of names and personal histories of people who claimed to be liberal teachers, writers, or political prisoners, weeding out the phonies. Many criminals from the 999th tried to appear to be like their more intellectual comrades, but none slipped through the screening.

"Everyone would say he was a professor or a political leader when he might be a murderer," Kunzig remembers. "We had a problem finding out. Usually, we could corroborate. If he was a famous professor, you could find someone at Brown or Princeton or Michigan who'd say, 'Oh, yes, I've heard of him.' Then you'd put things together and weed it out."

None of the Factory men were ever promised anything by

the army, although it was hoped that they would be repatriated first to help with the occupation. One, however, did receive some concessions because of his personal history as well as his Factory contributions: Dr. Gustav René Hocke, the prizewinning German writer and novelist who was editor-in-chief of *Der Ruf* at Fort Kearney. Dr. Hocke, having fled the Gestapo, was a member of the anti-Fascist underground in Rome and served— under duress— as a civilian interpreter for the German Army in Sicily. After his capture, he worked for the Allies writing anti-Nazi leaflets until a general internment order forced his transfer to a POW camp.

When he reached the United States, Dr. Hocke refused to be placed in a camp with Nazis. Eventually he was transferred to Fort Kearney. Although the United States never followed up on a 1946 promise by the provost marshal general "to invite me to the U.S.A. as a free man" ("I am still waiting for the invitation," he says), the SPD did make a special arrangement for him.

Hocke's wife, an Englishwoman, and his son had been in England since 1939. On January 11, 1946, after months of negotiations with the British, Hocke was transferred to Wilton Park, England, to edit *Die Wochenpost*, a publication similar to *Der Ruf*, and to be with his family. He was possibly the only prisoner of war to be moved to a country other than that of his nationality or one in whose army he had "served." (Postwar correspondence indicates that the other men at Kearney did not know of Hocke's good fortune.)

The first step at the Factory was the equalization of all the prisoners. The officers among them renounced their Wehrmacht rank to make it clear that everyone would do his share. After a few weeks all the jobs were assigned and the first reeducation work— *Der Ruf* and translations into German of teaching aids—began.

The eighty-five men were divided into six sections to handle these jobs: translation of POW newspapers into English and reeducation material into German; review of POW camp newspapers; review of plays, music, and books to determine whether

they should be available to POWs; review of films to determine
whether they were politically and culturally appropriate to be
persuasive to German POWs; publication of *Der Ruf*; and administration of the Factory. In addition, they were to prepare themselves to be repatriated and hopefully to assume key roles either
in the military government or in the political reeducation of all
Germany. (As a memo to Davison from Walter Schoenstedt read
in 1945: "It is of utmost importance to conduct the political
reeducation of all Germans, whenever possible, by Germans
under constant guidance. . . . Therefore, it is suggested that
arrangements be made for the transfer of an essential part of 'The
Factory' to the American Zone of Occupation in Germany.")

The administrative section was headed by the camp's
spokesman, who had responsibility for the supervision and welfare of the prisoners. He was assisted by a prisoner clerk-typist
and a prisoner engineering technician who was responsible for
the facilities. A prisoner acting first sergeant supervised maintenance. Approximately 10 percent of the men were assigned to no
specific section. They used the facilities as needed for individual
projects or to assist others.

A director of studies selected by the prisoners organized and
supervised leisure-time activities for the internees at Fort Kearney. He also organized English-language classes and assisted the
compound commander in coordinating the work of the six
sections.

By far the most important mission of the Factory was the
publication of *Der Ruf*, a biweekly newspaper of about eight
pages. (The War Department called it a magazine, but its physical
format was that of a newspaper.) The *Der Ruf* section of the
Factory—Dr. Hocke, Curt Vinz, and others—spent their first
two weeks on plans and policies for the paper. The PMG's office
theoretically supervised the paper, but the contents did not voice
official U.S. opinion. *Der Ruf*, according to the War Department, was to be a prisoner-of-war magazine that would give
cultural and moral support to the prisoners, who were naturally

expected to be depressed and lost after Germany's defeat. Most important, it was "to foster traditions based on the principles of right, independent thinking, decency, personal freedom and the Four Freedoms."

The first issue appeared in camp canteens on March 6, 1945. Nazi groups immediately tried to prevent its distribution. They bought all the copies and burned them or threatened dire consequences to anyone caught reading one.

Signs like this one at Camp Perry, Ohio, appeared in many camps:

> *Kameraden! Glauben die Amerikaner dass wir uns eine Zeitung von Verrätern and Uberlaufer aufdringen lassen? Ihr kennt nun alle Der Ruf!*
>
> *Sollen wir uns durch die Bilder unseres Köln und Trier verhöhnen lassen? Will man uns sagen, wir müssen die verlorene Ehre wiedergewinnen? Boykottiert! Diese schändliche Zeitung! Washington will mit uns "ein Experiment machen!" (New York Times).*
>
> *Unsere Ehre aber heisst Treue, unser Glaube Deutschland! JETZT ERST RECHT!*

(Translation: "Do the Americans believe they can force upon us a newspaper of traitors and deserters? All of you know by now *Der Ruf*! Shall we allow the pictures of Cologne and Trier to mock us? Do they want to tell us that we must regain our lost honor? *Boycott*! This shameful newspaper! Washington wants to 'make an experiment' of us! (*New York Times*). But our honor means faith, our belief Germany! NOW MORE THAN EVER!")

But gradually *Der Ruf* and the reaction to it became both an excellent means for determining the attitudes of the prisoners in light of the reeducation program and a helpful addition to the program.

Although only eleven thousand copies were printed of the first edition, by the fifteenth issue, seventy-five thousand copies were being run. Ninety percent of each edition was sold. The paper was solvent, since it cost only three and a half cents to print each copy and the canteen price was five cents. (The price of the eleventh issue was dropped to four cents, and the twelfth to sixteenth editions sold for two and a half cents each.) The division had elected to sell it rather than give it away because they felt the prisoners would be less suspicious of anything that they had to purchase.

Der Ruf was a very highbrow German-language publication. As SPD members joked, it was "a newspaper which even Thomas Mann would find difficult to understand. This was a great success among the prisoners, because it seems the Germans believe that anything they can't understand must be pretty hot stuff."

One reason for its caliber was to make it appear to be a regular German newspaper. Kunzig says, "German newspapers are very specialized things. Though nowadays they have more of that sexy scare stuff like we have, a lot of them are very high-level, with an intellectual-article column, one which may contain a long analysis of something. German writers do an awful lot of what we would call editorializing. *Der Ruf* was a very high-level thing. It didn't look interesting, but it was what they were used to reading. We carried some war news, because eventually they believed this thing. My general memory is that it became very much believed. The people felt they had been lied to, and they believed this—it looked like home."

The first edition of *Der Ruf* had two front-page stories. The first, a lengthy article entitled "*Die Inneren Mächte*" ("The Inner Power"), discussed the human soul and the idea that the shape of the world was not the fault of the average man. It referred liberally to passages from Goethe, Schiller, Schopenhauer, and other German philosophers. The second was entitled "*Der Ruf an die deutschen Kriegsgefangenen in Amerika*" ("The Call to the German Prisoners of War in America"). It described *Der Ruf* as "the call from the homeland."

Inside pages included articles on Field Marshal Karl von Rundstedt's receipt of the Ritter Cross (and British Field Marshal Bernard Montgomery's comment that von Rundstedt was the best enemy general); the situation in Europe, including the Yalta and Tehran conferences; the current battlefronts in Europe (stating frankly that Germany was losing); news from the Reich (mostly about destruction from Allied bombing and its effects); a Viennese song; and a good news section entitled "The White Sails," which mentioned Albert Schweitzer's seventieth birthday and memories of happier days at home. A literature section discussed the value of the Nobel prize for literature and its first winner (a Dane) and included a review of Stephen Vincent Benét's book *America*, published in 1944. The latter was written with the intention of acquainting the POWs with the United States and American hopes and dreams. There was also a music section which covered the Metropolitan Opera season in New York.

A lengthy section discussed the economy of the Southern states and their cotton and fruit industries. It also explained the history and geography of the South and the roots of slavery.

The final portion, letters to the editor, contained seven letters allegedly from prisoners. They included comments on camp sports, going to church, how to make a violin, and a suggestion for an excellent book to read: *The Late George Apley*, by J. P. Marquand.

Later editions ventured more brazenly into reeducation. For example, the seventeenth edition, November 15, 1945, had articles discussing true patriotism for a German and suggesting city planning in the postwar world. There were others on the effects of dictatorship on the middle class, Austria, and *die geistige Kluft* ("the spiritual gap") in Germany. Prisoner letters and free-lance contributions were encouraged.

Reaction to the early editions was mixed. Not all prisoners were easily sold on *Der Ruf*. This was, after all, enemy territory, and all but the strongest anti-Nazis were suspicious and wary. One prisoner wrote home: "We receive here a prisoner paper. It is called 'Der Ruf' and they claim it's German. I would like to call it a paper printed with German words. This paper is clever and very subtle. One has to read it a few times until one finds that it is supposed to be political reeducation for us. But we are Nazis and we will remain Nazis and only laugh about it."

Prisoners at Camp Somerset, Maryland, felt that it was "too obvious" and responded to it as propaganda. At Camp Alva, Oklahoma, a segregation center for ardent Nazis, there was strong resistance to the publication, and Camp Beale, California, was one of many camps which reported problems in circulating the paper. Yet, at Camp Plauch, Louisiana, the SPD gloated that even though the Nazi clique prevented the publication of the camp's own paper, *Der Ruf* was having an effect on the men.

Kunzig admits that the effects of the newspaper were gradual: "In the original days of *Der Ruf*, it was a mortal sin to be caught reading it. Later on, everybody read it, and it was a very, very successful high-level indoctrination. Really it was indoctrination by correct facts. They weren't used to correct facts and didn't believe what they saw in *Der Ruf* until time proved how right the magazines were and how wrong their communiqués were."

Curt Vinz, the German publisher who was one of the editors of *Der Ruf* and of a series of books published at the Factory, feels that German morale had hit a very low ebb, "but the publishing of *Der Ruf* and the *Neue Welt* series rekindled interest in literature" and, thus, in reading generally.

Evidence tends to support the Kunzig-Vinz opinion on the success of *Der Ruf*. At the same camp from which the Nazi wrote the letter condemning the paper, the assistant executive officer (AEO), only a few weeks later, sent a note to the SPD: "Request that you send us at least fifty (50) additional copies of each printing of 'Der Ruf.' "

Der Ruf was an important addition to the reeducation program for many reasons. It provided an easy way for the SPD officers placed in each camp to gauge Nazi strength and pick out its advocates, since the true Nazis boycotted the publication. It also influenced the eighty local camp papers: a study showed that after *Der Ruf* began, the camp papers became less Nazi and more nonpolitical. (The original count of thirty-three clearly Nazi and three anti-Nazi papers became twenty-four democratic, eighteen anti-Nazi, and only one openly Nazi.) Nazi symbols disappeared from the pages of most camp papers.

The army did a survey of reactions to the first five editions, and as a result, necessary adjustments were made. By the fall of 1945, Colonel Davison could claim, with credibility, that the combination of *Der Ruf* and the fledgling reeducation courses was having a noticeable and increasing effect on the camp population. Immediately distinguishable were the decreasing number of eulogies to German military or political heroes, the end of the glorification of *Kameradschaft* ("comradeship") for political unity, the ending of *Morgenfeiern*, less self-pity, fewer disparaging remarks about the United States and its allies, an end to pan-German propaganda in camps where men of other nationalities were also interned, and the end of pseudopsychological articles in camp papers justifying German brutality.

Many of these changes were discerned through the monitoring of camp papers at the Factory. The publications, usually simple mimeographed leaflets of eight or ten sides in length, were reviewed regularly by a section of the Factory to detect Nazi influence and the effects of reeducation, if any, on their content.

The division, with the help of Factory residents, put out a guide suggesting ideal contents for camp newspapers. It recommended that the papers be used as a medium for self-education and a source for factual information, that the editors be impartial and objective, that reprints of German and Allied communiqués be balanced, that quotations from works of certain German authors be encouraged, and that the papers include forums to provide for the voice of the majority (presumably non-Nazi) which would be coordinated with educational activities.

In June 1945, the SPD decided to have the men at the Factory begin publishing a biweekly clipsheet to supplement *Der Ruf*. Since there was little intercamp communication, the clipsheet, *Die Auslese* ("The Selection"), was designed to fill the gap. Prisoners at Fort Kearney chose articles from various camp papers to reprint in *Die Auslese* along with translations of Office of War Information (OWI) releases.

Articles were selected to emphasize the destruction of Nazi doctrines and practices, the positive aspects of pre-Hitler Germany, new democratic tendencies, and American democracy. The first issue, with a press run of two thousand, appeared July 21, 1945. It never received the acceptance of *Der Ruf* because it was too obvious a vehicle for propaganda.

Publications were only the beginning. The army, worried that the camp schools would be breeding grounds for Nazism, altered these schools after V-E Day. Efforts to eliminate courses of no value to reeducation had begun months before, but as of V-E Day all classes preparatory for work in the German civil service were canceled and a minimum essential program of English, history, geography, and other classes conducive to the democratic point of view was stressed.

Preparing material for the revamped schools and reviewing books to be used in the classes and libraries in anticipation of the changes fell to the Factory. Through the diligent efforts of the select prisoners and the SPD, Nazi views would virtually disappear from reading and teaching by the end of May 1945.

At the Factory the men concentrated on two areas: censorship and translations. Under the heading of censorship, the men would read, analyze, and evaluate all books being considered for use in classes, on library shelves, and for sale in canteens. For example, they rated the book *Children in the U.S.A.* and declared it suitable for all POWs. Karl K., one of the reviewers, wrote: "The small book would be extremely valuable in the reeducation of German PWs. It gives in very good pictures and in short articles a general idea how the American child grows up. The majority of all PWs are eager to learn about 'the American way of living.' Here they can receive some of that knowledge.

"It seems advisable to use the word 'Democracy' only very seldom in the accompanying text. These small changes could be easily done without changing the idea of the book."

So that great quantities of educational and literary material of an anti-fascist nature could flow into the camps, a plan was devised to produce a series of books entitled *Bücherreihe Neue Welt* ("New World Books"). This series was also a product of the Factory.

Curt Vinz remembers the *Neue Welt* books particularly clearly:

Among the 24 volumes published under Neue Welt were mostly works from exiles of Hitler's Germany like Leonhard Frank, Franz Werfel, Arnold Zweig and Carl Zuckmayer. Thomas Mann was represented in four volumes, with a two-volume edition taken from *The Magic Mountain, Lotte in Weimar* and essays *Attention Europe*. Translated into German for this series were works of Stephen Vincent Benét, Joseph Conrad, William Saroyan and Ernest Hemingway, whose novel *For Whom The Bell Tolls* had the most effect on the prisoners of war not only because of the war theme but because of the new writing style (for Germans) of short, direct dialogue, understatement and realism.

For legal reasons, the *Infantry Journal* was considered the publisher of the *Neue Welt* series, but the copyright belonged to Bermann-Fischer Verlag, Thomas Mann's German publisher, who was in exile in Sweden. Later Dr. Gottfried Bermann-Fischer noted in his memoirs, *Bedroht—Bewahrt* [Threatened —Saved], that he had made an arrangement that later proved the basis for a new, profitable series of books. He wrote: "My connection with Herr Vinz was very productive. The selection from the specially requested list of books was obtained easily, and a series of books under the name *Neue Welt*, with a first edition of 50,000 copies was published in early 1945, before the end of the war, and was in very short time sold to the prisoners of war. That was the beginning of what was later to become the Fischer Library."

Bermann-Fischer Verlag received royalty payments of one cent for every copy of the *Neue Welt* books sold in the canteens.

After the success of the *Neue Welt* series, the division had the Factory translate several books into German which were more overtly designed to combat Nazism. The first was entitled *Kleiner Führer durch Amerika* ("Brief Guide to America") and was issued to each prisoner as a souvenir and basic text.

Three pamphlets written by Howard Mumford Jones specifically for reeducation were translated and circulated in the summer of 1945. They were *Eine Einführung in das amerikanische Schule* ("A Brief Survey of American Schools"), *Eine Einführung in die amerikanische Verfassung und Verwaltung* ("A Brief Survey of American Government"), and *Kurze Geschichte der Vereinigten Staaten* ("A Short History of the United States").

One education aid which the SPD employed very successfully it may have learned from the Nazis—the effective use of films for propaganda. Films were shown in the camps regularly as part of prisoner recreation, and were paid for by canteen earnings. Prior to the reeducation program, the films were selected by the camp spokesman, who was usually a tool of the Nazi leadership. The films they selected were designed to support Nazi propaganda, which labeled the Americans as "senile," and depicted rampant gangsterism, corruption, and the debilitating effect of democracy. Early camp favorites were *Lady Scarface, Seven Miles from Alcatraz, Legion of the Lawless*, and similar wholesome productions.

It was obvious something had to be done. The army wanted the POWs to see films which reflected America "without distortion" and fostered respect for democracy. The OWI compiled

catalogues of 16mm feature films, documentaries, and educational films. The men at the Factory screened hundreds of films—
features, short subjects, and travelogues—to weed out the undesirable ones. They eliminated from the list all films depicting
gangsters or prison life; those ridiculing any ally; those misrepre-
senting the American scene by stressing the plutocratic aspects;
"hot" musicals; films containing Depression and slum scenes,
racial slurs, or strife between capital and labor; blood-and-
thunder cowboy pictures; and films of unrealistic Hollywood
scenes.

Films that seemed too propagandistic or too "mushy" were
also dropped on the recommendation of the Germans at the
Factory. It was the firm rejection by Factory members of the
propaganda film *Tomorrow the World* that prevented its being
shown to prisoners. The Germans felt that the small boy depicted
as the product of Hitlerism was overdone and not even the worst
Nazi environment could have fathered him. They also argued
that the American, played by Fredric March, was too soft-
hearted and too easily duped to reflect credit on the American
system among the prisoner corps.

On the approved list after screening were movies which,
according to the SPD, "more truly reflected the American
scene." Films dealing with family life, common human experiences, drama, wholesome comedy, good musicals, adaptations of
fine plays, realistic "action" pictures, contemporary or historical
topics, documentaries, travelogues, film histories, and biog-
raphies were approved. After Germany started losing heavily on
the battlefield, the film attack picked up, and propaganda films
and those depicting atrocities in concentration camps were added
to the list.

Among the feature films deemed appropriate for POWs
were *Abe Lincoln in Illinois, The Adventures of Mark Twain, The
Adventures of Tom Sawyer, Back to Bataan, Courageous Mr.
Penn, Captain Eddie, King of Kings, Guadalcanal Diary, Land
of Liberty, Madame Curie, Sign of the Cross, Song of Berna-*

dette, The Story of Alexander Graham Bell, The Human Comedy, How Green Was My Valley, Lost Horizon, The Aldrich Family, Christmas in July, Young Mr. Lincoln, and all the *Andy Hardy* films.

An OWI series of films called *This Is America* and OWI documentaries like *Swedes in America* and *T.V.A.* were also shown. In his analysis of the *Why We Fight* series of OWI propaganda films, Factory screener Oskar W. concluded that "the documentary film serves the prisoners as finger-pointing to a future which will be hard but nevertheless worth living for, and it will educate them to become valid members in the community of nations."

In order that the POWs could not claim they were being permitted only American films, two old German films were also on the approved list, since they predated Nazi influence on the medium. Copies of the two, *Ein Prinz Verliebt Sich [A Prince in Love with Himself]* and Schubert's *Frühlingstraum [Spring Dream]*, were in plentiful supply but really could not compete with the American films for prisoner popularity, since the POWs soon recognized Hollywood's technical superiority. Most films were not subtitled or dubbed, and the Factory prepared a German synopsis of each to be distributed at the door.

The Factory could not have arranged distribution or permission to show the films with the support of the studios. For that, the Special Projects Division brought in two Hollywood experts, Captain Otto Englander and Lieutenant James E. Stewart. Unfortunately, the War Department decided that individual camps or the SPD should not make their own arrangements. The whole army got involved. The Motion Picture Service would purchase the films, the Signal Corps would book them, and the SPD would merely select the films and see that the camps used them. It was a predictable mess.

It took the army until March 1945, six months after the rest of the program got started, before its bureaucracy decided how it would handle the financial side. Englander spent months trying to mediate and get the program off the ground. SPD members teased him profusely:

> Captain E. made a special visit to Washington to confer with a variety of echelons concerning the problems of getting films into PW camps, films which publicized neither Gertie's garter nor Tom Mix's horse. Although higher echelons agreed on the desirability of the undertaking, they couldn't agree on who should get the profits. As a result, Captain E. spent most of his time during the following six months on trains between New York and Washington, and although he oriented few prisoners, it is understood that he eliminated all race prejudice among Pullman porters on this run.

In addition, there was initial antagonism to the idea among the Hollywood moguls because of the insistence that the reeducation program be top secret. After all, most of the big producers were not of an ethnic background that looked kindly upon Germans in 1944. Maxwell McKnight explains: "The big problem was the Hollywood Jewish group. I'm sorry to say that word, but they had a lot of problems when they found out their films were used to 'coddle' German POWs. Finally the secretary of war had to call in all the Warner Brothers people—the key ones—and explain what was being done and that it was a secret program. Once they understood that there was a program to take advantage of a half-million Germans—to denazify them, to use a Flit gun—then, of course, we got enormous cooperation."

To the credit of everyone in the SPD, the program ran well once it started. Studies showed that 130 base camps and 243 branch camps had achieved significant prisoner interest, access to good equipment, funds, and projectionists in sufficient quantity to make the film program successful.

In all, 450 films were reviewed at the Factory, and 115 were approved. The SPD estimated in late 1945 that the average prisoner had seen ten approved feature films.

Although Factory members spent less time reviewing and working on other educational materials, music, art, and theater, considered "minor media," were not ignored. They translated Norman Corwin's "On a Note of Triumph" radio show into German and circulated eight copies to the camps for use over the public-address system. They also helped in obtaining more than a thousand music records for use over the loudspeakers. The Nazis had used military marches and militaristic folk songs as primary musical pieces for daily consumption. In the theaters, painted or carved swastikas and slogans adorned the stages. Pseudotheatrical presentations were also used to push the party line. This was difficult to control in the camps because Americans knew little of traditional German music, art, or theater.

Texts of plays, entertainment bills of fare, concert selections, and all other cultural choices of POWs were forwarded to the Factory, where the Germans could evaluate whether they were Nazi-oriented. Factoryites also selected works by Jews and blacks for introduction into the camps. German-language explanations were written to accompany these works, stressing the writer or composer and comparing them with "Aryan" works.

A subsidiary job at the Factory was making recommendations for postwar Europe, for Germany in particular. Several prisoners wrote long papers on specific topics. Whether any of them were ever acted upon is impossible to ascertain. Some topics included radio programming in Germany ("Keep military music strictly from the air"), the press in Germany, a medical school for POWs based on the expected need for health care in defeated Germany, housing, city reconstruction, and the importance of educational-exchange fellowships to reeducation in Germany.

On July 6, 1945, a commencement exercise was held at Kearney at which each man was given a certificate of achievement for completing the "training course for prisoners of war." For eight weeks, in addition to their other duties, most of the men had been taking classes to prepare them to work for the

military government and to educate fellow-Germans about democratic government.

The school was a pilot project for the SPD, which hoped to
expand the concept of teaching other special German prisoners at
a school about to be established at Fort Getty, Rhode Island.
Sixty residents of the Factory were chosen as guinea pigs. The
experiment was an overwhelming success. Of their ability as
students, T. V. Smith reported: "I hazard the guess that these
Germans have a better command of English after two months
than the average of our American officers had of a foreign language at Charlottesville [American Military Government School]
after four months."

In his commencement address to the prisoners, which discussed the problems ahead in reconstructing Germany, Howard
Mumford Jones concluded by saying:

> It may seem odd to appeal to the spirit of a prison camp and
> of a military installation, but what is the idea behind Fort
> Kearney unless it is the notion of human dignity and of the
> brotherhood of man? When therefore I say to you it is my
> hope, as it is the hope of other members of this faculty, of the
> officers of this post, and of your fellow prisoners . . . that
> the spirit of Fort Kearney may go with you wherever you
> are, I speak for these, your associates, as well as for myself,
> no less than for the American government which has sanc-
> tioned this amazing enterprise. May you be, each one, a
> good Christian soldier in the campaign against hatred and ill
> will.

The list of names of the first bloc of Kearney men to be
repatriated was released on September 11, 1945. It included Vinz
and nine others. In all, the list named two journalists, two illus-
trators, an artist, an educator, a publisher, an editor, a composer,
and a trade teacher—all men of potential value to the occupation.
The same day, in a letter to Brigadier General Robert A.

McClure, Director of the Information Control Division in the office of U.S. Military Government in Germany, Provost Marshal General Lerch wrote that the prisoners "have expressed willingness to keep on working under the supervision of American military authorities after repatriation," and added, "No promises have been made to these prisoners regarding an assignment, but I do hope that, in case they are able to contact your organization, it will be possible to give them an interview."

The last two days at the Factory were hectic. Kunzig remembers: "Suddenly we got orders that the first group was to go back to Germany. The big problem was, nobody ever thought of new clothes. They were all in blue denims or green—whichever—and fatigues. The big problem was what to do. I called Howard McGrath and said we had this horrible problem. He was very helpful, and through certain agencies, within about twenty-four hours, they dug up all sorts of clothes—mismatched junk, but clothes. I can still see the scene where we spread out all these clothes all over the whole place and each person would pick a suit or a pair of pants or a shirt or something that fit him. Ill-fitting, but at least it would cover his nakedness, and off they went back to Germany the next day."

As Maxwell McKnight once wrote to Colonel Davison: "No one visits Kearney without coming away with the feeling that they had an exciting experience." The Factory, as the hub of the reeducation program, was a vital, active place. But, obviously, it could not do it alone. To properly use their material and see that the goals of the SPD were achieved, a man had to be assigned to every POW camp to supervise what the War Department euphemistically called "intellectual diversion."

The SPD felt that to do the job right it needed nine company-grade officers to supply each service command with an administrator, and field-grade officers as assistant executive officers (AEOs)—the men who would be placed in the individual camps. These men were expected to be experts on journalism and films and on American and German literature. They needed previous experience in POW camps and in education, and a fluency in German. Obviously, to fill all these requirements was not an easy order.

The original hope was to get 150 officers. To accomplish this, Davison and his staff set about reviewing hundreds of files and selected men by name. This proved fruitless because most of the best men had already been absorbed by the planned Allied Military Government and Military Institute. So, the three military commands were ordered to send personnel, and the German-language requirement was dropped in order to concentrate on the other, more important needs.

The first groups began orientation at three conferences held at Fort Slocum, New York, in November and December 1944 and January 1945. (The last AEO training conference was held in May 1945.)

One new AEO, Cumins Speakman, remembered the reactions of his fellow-students as their training began. "There was a feeling of excitement among the officers gathered at Fort Slocum," he wrote, "as the full scope of the program was revealed to them." Each man selected for AEO training was assigned an adviser and given a comprehensive examination and a hypothetical study on the orientation of POWs. During a week-long conference they attended lectures, discussions, or seminars on twenty-six subjects and toured a POW camp.*

A total of 262 officers and 111 enlisted men were eventually sent to the service commands for the purpose of heading camp

---

*Among the twenty-six topics were Administration; Intelligence and Security Clearance; the Mission and Background of the Program; German History; German Education; German Army; Educational Activities in POW Camps; Field Problems; Review of Publications; Book Procurement; POW Chaplain Activities; POW Intellectual Activities; *Der Ruf* and Camp Publications; Staff Functions and Visiting Organizations; Film as a Medium—Nazi Film Propaganda; Public Relations; German Propaganda; Psychology of Prisoners of War; Psychology of the German; Orientation of Guards; Other Media (Art, Music, Theater, Radio); "We or They?"—Ideology of the Two Worlds; Anticipated V-E Day Problems; Introduction to Staff Study; Role of the State Department; POW Administration; and Security of Prisoner-of-War Camps.

reeducation programs. (The officers were AEOs, and the enlisted men their aides.) Enough men had been trained to staff all of the base camps (approximately 160) and one-fourth of the branch camps (variable, but about 400).

Although G1 wrote to Mrs. Roosevelt in late 1944 reporting on their great progress, the natural problems at the start of any program were magnified by a striking lack of coordination within the War Department. The newly assigned AEO at Camp Butner, North Carolina, wrote in a later report:

> I assumed of course that the Service Command or Washington had informed the camp of the impending arrival of an AEO but was soon to learn that the basis of the warm welcome was the shortage of officers and an addition to the OD roster. Instructions from Service Command did not come for several weeks. Meantime I had to explain to the Commanding Officer the background, organization, aims and media of the program. Following his advice I began to acclimate by osmosis. The result of the first two weeks included a desk, files, two chairs, and a dawning comprehension of the organization and operation of a POW camp.

At least he had hit a CO who was cooperative. Many AEOs were not even that lucky and met with strong opposition. At Fort Lewis, Washington, for example, the program was late getting off the ground because the commanding officer did not believe such a plan had any place in his camp. The CO heaped mounds of his own work on the AEO to obstruct his ability to give time to reeducation. When the AEO refused to do the work, the CO attempted to have him reassigned as a "troublemaker." An SPD investigating committee reported that the program "took a shellacking" because of the "obdurate, stupid, narrow-minded so-and-so of a camp commander." It was the CO who found himself transferred.

Although several Jews were brought in as AEOs and

advisers, the SPD worried about the German reaction to dealing with members of that faith. They soon discovered that Jewish AEOs were having more trouble with fellow-officers in the camps than with the POWs. At one camp the Jewish AEO finally had to be replaced by a Gentile because the anti-Semitic CO, along with other officers, was hindering his work by encouraging the Germans and American enlisted personnel to ignore the AEO's directions.

Generally, though, the AEOs settled in within a few weeks and began their task. The original plan called for only the most cooperative prisoners "selected by scrupulous screening" to receive "higher education of a liberal character." The steps laid down in that plan were merely a beginning. The actual program was never "select"; the SPD went much further, by deciding to reeducate everyone.

Under the expanded concept, the role of the AEO in the individual camps was crucial. The success or failure of reeducation in each camp depended on his energy and imagination. The AEOs' techniques and goals became more ambitious as the project progressed.

Top, *Prisoners of War Special Projects Division officers at Fort Getty, R.I., graduation, November 30, 1945. From left, front row, Lieutenant Commander Edwin Casady, Captain Meyer, M.D., Lieutenant Colonel Edward Davison, Lieutenant Colonel Alpheus Smith, Major Henry Lee Smith, Jr.* (U.S. Army Photo. From Moulton Papers)

Bottom, *Graduation from Fort Getty (Administrative School), November 30, 1945.* (U.S. Army Photo. From Moulton Papers)

Left, *Lieutenant Colonel Alpheus Smith, commandant of Fort Getty School and, later, of Fort Eustis, Virginia, School, 1945.* (U.S. Army Photo. From Moulton Papers)

Below, *Edwin Casady (now a full commander) teaches a discussion section at Fort Eustis.* (U.S. Army Photo. From Moulton Papers)

Opposite top, *Major Maxwell S. McKnight speaking at Fort Benning, Georgia, meeting for AEOs and select prisoners on reeducation, October 29–November 1, 1945.* (U.S. Army Photo. From McKnight Papers)

Opposite bottom, *Compound School, Camp Mackall, North Carolina, a reeducation class taught by an anti-Nazi POW director of studies, 1945.* (U.S. Army Photo)

Opposite and above, *Reeducation studies at Fort Benning, Georgia, taken from* Wille und Weg, *the booklet prepared for the October, 1945, reeducation conference.*

Above and opposite, *Pages from the booklet* Wille und Weg, *showing some of the subjects studied and the approach used. All are typical of the course materials used in the reeducation program.*

DIE RECHTS-UND GESETZES-ORGANE
THE · AGENCIES · OF · JUSTICE · AND · LAW ·

VERFASSUNG

U.S. OBERSTER GERICHTSHOF

U.S. BERUFUNGS-GERICHT

U.S. DISTRIKT-GERICHTE

ZUM SCHUTZ DES VOLKES

Oberster Staatsanwalt
für die Nation

Staatsanwalt
für den Staat

Bezirksanwalt
für die Bezirke

Gemeindeanwalt
für die Stadt

Öffentlicher Verteidiger
für Mittellose

Oberster Gerichtshof des Staates

Berufungsgericht des Staates

Grafschafts-Gerichte

POLIZEI

Bundes-Polizei
Gemeindedienst
u.s.w.

Staats-Polizei

Orts-Polizei

Der Vorfahre unseres Rechtswesens...
der königliche Gerichtshof

... und die Ausübung des Rechts im heutigen Amerika.

Friedensrichter
für leichte Fälle

Stadt- und Bezirks-Gerichte
für schwerere Fälle

Verkehrsgericht

Jugendgericht

DAS VOLK UND DAS GEMEINE GESETZ = DIE GRUNDLAGE DES BAUES

DIE FREIHEITSURKUNDE (1791)
THE · BILL · OF · RIGHTS · GUARANTEES · THESE · FUNDAMENTALS ·

VERBÜRGT FOLGENDE GRUNDRECHTE UND FREIHEITEN

DIE FREIHEIT:

▸ der Religion

▸ der Rede
und Presse

▸ des Heimes
der Person
des Eigentums

▸ von zu hohen Bürgschaften
zu hohen Geldstrafen
grausamen und ungewöhn-
lichen Strafen

DAS RECHT:

▸ auf gerechte Behand-
lung vor Gericht

▸ zu Versammlungen und
zur Berufung

▸ auf gerechte Vergütung
für Enteignung von
Gut für öffentliche Zwecke

▸ auf richtige Befolgung
des Gesetzes

▸ Waffen zu halten und zu-
tragen

▸ Die Erhaltung der Rechte des Volkes

SIEBZEHNTES JAHRHUNDERT 1700 ACHTZEHNTES JAHRHUNDERT
1610 1620 1630 1640 1650 1660 1670 1680 1690 1700 1710 1720 1730 1740 1750 1760 1770 1780 1790

Above, *At the police school, Strobel, Austria, June, 1946. The students are former special projects prisoners of war.* (U.S. Army Photo)

5 Intellectual Diversion Program

The terms "reeducation" or "reorientation" of
prisoners of war will not be used in referring
to the mission of this Branch. The term "I.D. Program"
(Intellectual Diversion) will be used whenever
reference is made to the program.

—Office Memo Number 4 from Edward Davison,
September 22, 1944

THE ASSISTANT EXECUTIVE OFFICERS discovered as soon as they
began work that many camps fit the description they had studied
at Fort Slocum. Most found a few "Holy Ghost" incidents had
occurred, American newspapers and magazines were rarely read,
and the Nazis controlled the schools and prevented political
discussion. The AEOs were ready to meet the challenge, but how
could they do so without being obvious?

They had been told during training that the War and State
departments preferred that the SPD stay on safe ground by
running a limited program of "indoctrination by example." But it

had been clear to SPD mentors from the start that such a program would not work. There was too much Nazi pressure on their fellow-prisoners to reject friendly, honest, and humane American advances, as the AEOs learned immediately.

"Only by judicious emphasis on choice of materials going into POW camps and right emphasis in their use and in the directions taken by education courses and recreational activities" could there be effective orientation, the SPD had stressed. The first thing the AEOs had to do was censor books and materials entering their camps. Their initial encounter with Nazi propaganda requiring censorship was in dealing with, of all groups, the German Red Cross.

The German Red Cross sent books, pamphlets, beautiful calendars, and even "religious" journals to the prisoners. All of them contained Nazi ideology, slogans, and warnings. The classic case was that of the Christmas packages which arrived in camp at about the same time as the first AEOs. That Yuletide, the GRC's gift to the prisoners contained, among other things, walnuts. All the walnuts were stuffed with propaganda messages. The content was "a mixture of about three parts deutsche Romantik and one part of political propaganda," according to an intelligence officer. The letter of Nazi law was conveyed by double entendre in poetic form. The officer summarized the message as: "You POWs over there keep your chins up; keep your mouths shut and stay in line politically or else." The walnuts were never distributed.

One of the other things the AEOs could do immediately was make a survey of the libraries, and gradually, so that it would appear to be regular rotation and avoid arousing suspicion, replace many of the books. They discarded "injurious" material, filled gaps, and estimated the popularity of given texts. Books by such authors as Alfred Rosenberg, Dr. Joseph Goebbels, Erich von Ludendorff, and dozens of other pro-Nazi or chauvinistic German writers began disappearing from the shelves.

The AEOs saw to it that the "proper" books were added in exchange. German classics, pre-Nazi fiction, books proscribed by the Nazis, and translations of English-language works found their way onto the shelves. Maxwell McKnight describes what slowly began to happen after that: "We got all the books banned in Germany and distributed them in the camps. And in the camps where they weren't burned by the Nazis, they were a real breakthrough, because all the years of the Nazis and their thought control were over. It was like opening a floodgate to nurse a Sahara."

Coincidentally, books priced from a few cents to several dollars appeared in the canteens. The *Neue Welt* series from the Factory, the *Encyclopaedia Britannica World Atlas* (priced at $12.50), and paperbacks like Nevins and Commager's *The Pocket History of the United States* went on sale. (The latter and some others were printed in both German and English editions.)

The AEO at Camp Butner, North Carolina, wrote about how he pored over catalogues and selected publications for his canteen to supplement those he was receiving from the SPD. He particularly liked photographic books that offered alluring pictures of the best the United States had to offer. He placed them for sale in the canteens noting: "We experimented in one side camp where there was some talk about 'propaganda.' A sign 'Souvenir Books of America' fixed that and sales boomed."

The AEOs were aware that their role had been carefully camouflaged. The Germans began looking upon them as combination special services officer, canteen officer, and assistant chaplain because of the many duties they performed, seemingly at the CO's bidding. These duties made it easier for them to move among the prisoners and get to know them. As Maxwell McKnight explains, "We put them there as assistant executive officers because they spoke German and the CO didn't. The Germans accepted this in terms of translating for the CO. It seemed to be a natural. No one suspected they were there to carry out a so-called reeducation program to open the camp to free information."

Hopefully, once they gained the POWs' confidence, the

AEOs would be able to make more changes. They knew that the army was chiefly concerned with the situation in the camp schools. After all, the schools were run by POW leaders. Many of the prisoner-teachers were either Nazis or had Nazi leanings. Numerous schools required reading from *Mein Kampf* and other Nazi texts. Gaining control of the schools was of major importance if the Intellectual Diversion Program was to succeed.

Each AEO had to find the right moment and method to move in on the schools in his own camp. But the AEOs weren't totally on their own—the war news was playing a bigger and bigger part as V-E Day approached. One turning point came when men captured on D-Day (June 6, 1944) began arriving and, at the suggestion of SPD members, were widely dispersed among the camps. McKnight reported: "When we invaded Normandy, the German prisoners were still riding high in the U.S., they still thought they were going to win the war. I remember meeting with General Bryan. I said, 'Look, we've got boatloads coming over. Why can't we use these prisoners who have just gone through the most horrendous experiences with the overwhelming Allied might—split them up. Send them to different camps as an addition to the reeducation program.' The reports we got were just absolutely fantastic. It broke the back of the Nazi hold. The COs reported to me that 'There was no singing in the mess hall last night.' The message was there."

AEOs used the shock of defeat and the growing confidence of anti-Hitlerite prisoners as the opening they needed. The AEO at Camp Concordia, Kansas, recorded: "From the beginning, small groups of officers had formed who were adverse to Nazism. While operating *sub rosa*, they were frequently able to counteract the efforts of the Nazi element. They did not oppose the Nazis openly. . . .

"The aim, rather, was to win the average prisoner to a more realistic thought-process without offending his patriotism, and to make them recognize, by their own efforts, the depths to which National Socialist doctrine had plunged Germany."

Having become aware of the covert democratic activities among the prisoners themselves, the AEO waited for the right moment to act. It came as the war news began turning heavily in favor of the Allied forces. Many nonpolitical prisoners wavered as the psychological effects of the impending German defeat engulfed them. The AEO recognized that the situation was reaching a crisis among the prisoners that had excellent potential from the American point of view. He quickly rounded up forty-four Nazi leaders and arranged for their immediate transfer to another camp.

The AEO, who had naturally been secretly supporting the camp's Anti-Nazi Privy Council, was now able to come out in the open to sponsor Intellectual Diversion activities. He wrote: "Pressure began to be exerted in a forceful manner so as to secure the complete dominance of the Anti-Nazi elements in the compounds. Things hitherto impossible were now freely undertaken."

Immediate objectives were removing the remaining subversive books from the library and personal possession of prisoners, reversing the editorial policy of the camp paper, creating a demand for *Der Ruf*, increasing church attendance, and discontinuing the regular camp university and replacing it with a school teaching exclusively English, American history, geography, and civics. Eighty-eight percent of the prisoners voluntarily attended the classes and purchased eight thousand books for "intellectual diversion" purposes. Shortly thereafter, a series of lectures on "intellectual diversion" subjects was begun "at the request of the Germans," with the result that over four thousand certificates of reeducation credits were later issued. Much of the work was done by the Germans themselves, with the AEO merely guiding and lecturing when requested.

At Camp Butner, the AEO faced a slightly different situation, which he readily capitalized on. Shortly after he arrived, the anti-Nazis were beginning to gain momentum in the wake of the disastrous war news. The Nazis retaliated with the usual threats

of physical violence. Eventually the target of their rantings became a particularly vocal anti-Nazi named Krudl.

One morning, posters appeared in the camp declaring,
"Comrades, beware of this man, a traitor to his Fatherland—
Krudl." The Nazi minority was reasserting its control by fear. The
AEO noted: "The next morning there was quite a hubbub. New
posters had been distributed in the night. 'Comrade, know you a
man who lives only for freedom and his Fatherland—Krudl.'"

Even those previously afraid to express a political opinion
joined in the growing discussion of Krudl's allegiance. The merits
of both sides were freely discussed, with proponents of each
speaking adamantly. Later, the AEO wrote: "Only three persons
at Camp Butner know the origin of those presumptuous follow-
up posters—the AEO who wrote them, the S-2 and the EM who
tacked them up at 0300 hours."

His ruse worked. The anti-Nazis suddenly discovered the
strength they really had in the camp. Control passed out of Nazi
hands. The AEO, after transferring a few of the worst Nazis to
another camp, was ready to revamp the school and begin "intellectual diversion."

How he wrested control was a matter each AEO had to solve
for himself. Once in a position of advantage, he had to work
diligently and yet cautiously to fit the school into the overall goals
of the program. The Nazi leadership had to be identified, broken,
and transferred to segregation areas. (This was often achieved
slowly, because of bureaucratic problems within each service
command.) A cooperative anti-Nazi or nonpolitical POW who
spoke English would become director of studies, and together
they would begin to reorganize or rearrange courses to emphasize
subjects needed for "intellectual diversion."

English became mandatory. Civics and geography jumped
to primary importance among elective courses. But the most
important area was American history.

American history was considered the best vehicle for teaching the democratic way of life—not by teaching history as history,

but by teaching history as a strategy of democratic living. The national story was told in its most dramatic and moral form: dramatic to keep the interest of the audience despite language problems, and moral to give them faith that what they learned would be applicable to the German condition.

To prevent the moral from becoming preachified and the dramatic from becoming ridiculous through too obvious showmanship, these elements were made logically organic to the course. "The conflicts of American way of life *are* drama on a cosmic scale, and the resolution of these conflicts (even the failure to resolve) *is* our national morality," Davison wrote in a memo to the SPD. The strategy was, therefore, to organize the course so as to let the pathos and logic of this American attempt at nation-building appear very clearly.

The subject was arranged topically (with a loosely chronological treatment of each part) and was treated as crisis-building and crisis-solving, letting the moral of the tale appear over and above our success (or lack thereof). Our two great failures (one by Britain, driving us to revolution, and the other our failure to solve problems leading to the Civil War) were treated as fully and fairly as our successes. Both were used to dramatize the nature and wisdom of tolerance and compromise.

Discussion periods held after lectures furthered this strategy by giving additional facts, by deepening the understanding of causes, by presenting illustrations to confirm or correct the lectures, or by answering questions in such a way as to provoke more discussion and thought.

Working on the assumption that Germans could be made excited about the new camp schools by the introduction of excellent examples of American higher education and possible college credit for themselves, the SPD expanded its activity.

McKnight recalls: "We lined up all the universities that we could get our hands on—and there were many. Wherever there was a camp, we got a university that normally had a German department, and we arranged for the university to send its Ger-

man-speaking head of the department and to open up its literature collections."

Over a hundred colleges and universities were asked to
cooperate with the AEOs in changing the classroom goals by
providing books and more extension courses for the POWs. One
of the plans for the revamped schools was to increase and encourage the number of students taking correspondence courses. As
the early Marshall-Paige-Davison plan judged: "The German has
a deep respect for education and should be given cause . . . to
respect American educational institutions."

The contribution of the University of Kansas to the program
at Camp Concordia was a particularly fine example. A large
proportion of the school's courses were accredited by the college,
and prior to the departure of the main body of officer prisoners in
September 1945, students with adequate academic achievements
received a certificate bearing the name of the university and the
signatures of some of its officials.

Not all camps did so well with university support. The AEO
at Camp Atlanta, Nebraska, complained frequently of the half-
hearted assistance he received from the University of Nebraska,
and the AEO at Fort Bliss, Texas, switched sponsors. Sul Ross
State Teachers College proved to be a much better benefactor
than the University of Texas School of Mines, which lacked the
liberal arts program that the Intellectual Diversion Program
demanded.

Overall, though, the program ran fairly well, and German
prisoners had the opportunity to take courses in "intellectual
diversion" related fields under the auspices of some of the most
distinguished American institutions.

In October 1944 the SPD decided to allow civilian lecturers,
usually professors from the participating colleges, to go into the
camps. Later, a few German refugees and approved teachers
from among the prisoners joined the list of traveling speakers.
The AEOs arranged for these men and representatives of the
army's speakers' bureau to give appropriate lectures.

Obviously, despite all the work that went on in the national headquarters of the POWSPD and the help from the colleges, the level of organization and success of the camp schools depended on the local AEO. The school at Fort Bragg, North Carolina, was typical of a successful program run by an able AEO. Beginning in July 1945, thirty-six themes were handled weekly, each taught six times so that all would have the opportunity to attend. The AEO estimated that 95 to 98 percent of the prisoners attended the sessions. Twenty-four of the topics were taught entirely in English.

General topic headings for the courses covered the predictable civics, American history, and geography. Individual themes were more exciting, varying from "The Bill of Rights" (civics) to "Jungle Yachts in the Belgian Congo" (geography). Emphasis was on the United States, with classes also available on South America, Africa, industrialization around the world, and some electives of POW interest, particularly agricultural science.

The outlines for the courses alone made a valuable reeducation booklet of ninety-four pages in length, to which a twenty-five-page camp-produced English textbook was added.

In a written examination given to 682 volunteers at Fort Bragg in November 1945, 5 percent received a rating of excellent in all three subjects—civics, American history, and English. Another 69 percent had scores of good or better. The AEO noted that the English program was having particular success. One way of judging this was "jokes in feature films in easy English provoke general laughter even if no explanation was given previously."

In a Gallup-style poll conducted at the camp, POWs were asked which of the subjects interested them the most. Civics was the overwhelming favorite, with 51 percent preferring it over the other subjects. Civics was also the area which was entirely new to 47 percent of the POWs. Three percent had never studied geography previously, and 28 percent had no prior knowledge of American history.

The AEO at Fort Bragg was very pleased with the results of

the program, as were army observers on the scene in late 1945. After "intellectual diversion" at Fort Bragg, 95 percent of the prisoners were familiar with American life and had a working knowledge of democracy. Prisoner Heinreid C., enthusiastic over the AEO's efforts, thanked him for the "magnificent opportunity to study political problems" that he had received in the United States.

Horst B. remarked that he was "impressed by the freedom of the press" that he learned of in the classes. Yet, "I was dismayed to find the horrible housing conditions for the working class," he said. "Provisions for old age pensions, and health insurance are very poor."

Representing the minority who were not sold by their lessons at Bragg, Hans S. commented: "You must not forget that we did try the so-called Democratic Way under Streseman and Bruening. [Gustav Streseman and Heinrich Bruening were chancellors of Germany during the doomed Weimar Republic, 1918-32.] It was a farce. . . . We cannot afford to have a lot of political parties milking the cow of Public Funds. With you it's different. You are rich and can afford a lot of nonsense which we just cannot. Where else in the world, could a nation support all the different pressure groups you have?" He had perhaps learned more about the American system than the SPD had intended.

At the other end of the scale were camps like Camp Croft, South Carolina, where in May 1945 there was still no evidence that the program was under way. The basic reason, according to the SPD, was the lack of segregation. Although Gestapo and SS men were identified among the prisoners, no action toward transfer of the clique could be obtained from the Fourth Service Command. Without segregation, the AEO could not make a dent.

Most camps fell somewhere between Fort Bragg and Camp Croft. Camp Somerset, Maryland, with 768 POWs, is a good example. It had a library of eight hundred volumes and an active school. Courses were taught in agriculture, biology, American history, American geography, civics, mechanics, music, German, French, Russian, bookkeeping, and, of course, English. The AEO had arranged the transfer of three ardent Nazis who had been hindering the program (two men who ridiculed readers of religious books, and a medic who demanded a *Heil* before he would give aid).

Segregation was the only sure way to neutralize Nazi dominance over their fellow-prisoners. After V-E Day it became more widely used, although never to the extent the AEOs would have liked. The most incorrigible Nazis—less than 10 percent—never succumbed to any efforts to reeducate them, though many other Nazis did. The segregation compound at Camp Butner, dubbed "Little Siberia," was an exclusive club for super-Nazis the AEO had nowhere else to send. They were kept completely apart from the main body of prisoners. But shortly after V-E Day even they became disillusioned with a losing cause and began participating in some "intellectual diversion" classes.

By the summer of 1945 the SPD was being forwarded many letters from converted POWs. Hans T., at Camp Bowie, Texas, wrote: "Believe me most of the Germans, who formerly promoted the poisonous and false propaganda are thinking differently today." But he suggested that if the United States would promise the Germans that the money they were earning would be theirs in cash after repatriation, reeducation would certainly be much more successful.

If the Intellectual Diversion Program was to be the success its planners hoped, it clearly could not be limited to the classroom. Central to the overall plan was the multimedia effort—approved newspapers, magazines, music, and films—that was being developed with the help of the Factory.

The film program, as the effort put into it by the SPD and the Factory indicates, was expected to be a major part of the program. AEOs received a rather lengthy list of things they were to do in promoting film use. Naturally, there were the obvious items—get projectors, screens, and so on. But more important was the planning of how to get the approved films into the camps.

The films had to be selected by free choice of the prisoners themselves so that they would not feel pressured or propagandized. (In addition to the Factory-approved list, AEOs could select equally appropriate films from local distributors.) A director of films was chosen from among the prisoners to make the choice of viewing fare for the camp.

Getting the Germans interested in the proper films after their pre-Intellectual Diversion diet of "X-rated" or German films took some doing. More ruses had to be adopted to get the program rolling. At Camp Butner, for example, the AEO wrote: "In December the PWs were being shown whatever German films were available because that was what they wanted. We knew, of course, that at best these films would be neutral or slightly antagonistic as far as the program was concerned. . . .

"We contracted for half a dozen of the oldest films in the German language we could get and followed them with Deanna Durbin in *It Started with Eve*. The next day the Spokesman asked us for more American films, about fifty-fifty."

Of course, there was the problem of language. Few of the films had German subtitles or dubbing, so a synopsis of the story had to be either read to the men before the show or distributed to them at the gate as they entered. Typical of many camps, Nazis at Butner would not allow the Factory-prepared synopses to be used. They insisted that the spokesman's Nazi interpreter do them.

The AEO reported:

When the first few stories were circulated they came back with many caustic remarks and corrections by budding critics along the route. Moreover, a note was directed to headquarters by the spokesman at one of the branch camps complaining of the inadequacy of the synopses. This suggested a bit of a coup that proved very successful.

The interpreter was bawled out by the AEO and told that if his work didn't improve he would be replaced by a more competent comrade. He was obviously shaken by the prospect of losing his pleasant job for a possible woodpulp or fertilizer plant detail and gulped appreciatively when one of our enlisted men offered to help him. And there was born a unique and profitable collaboration.

The interpreter was happy to listen and copy down word for word every sentence uttered by the solicitous American and then sign his own name to it.

Shortly thereafter, the AEO arranged for the commanding officer himself to compliment the prisoner on his improved work. That cinched it; the team would continue working together. The synopses became bolder, capitalizing on the positive elements of each film and ignoring—or perhaps misinterpreting—any unfavorable sequences.

AEOs were ordered to promote four specific types of films from the approved list: those demonstrating the democratic way of life at its best, those stressing heroism and achievements of democratic peoples (stories of Bell, Pasteur, Twain, Gunga Din, and so on), those showing the capacity for goodness and decency within the German people (for example, *The Seventh Cross*), and those demonstrating the brutal behavior of the Japanese (*The Good Earth, Back to Bataan*, and so on). Discussions were held after each showing to make sure the message had been received.

Films became such a popular source of diversion at many camps that, according to one former AEO, "their denial became a potent and practical disciplinary tool."

Emulating department-store holiday promotions, the POWSPD sent out a Christmas film catalogue to the camps in 1945 which reminded the AEOs: "Christmas is just around the corner, and it appears that we shall have a large number of the prisoners of war with us at that time. . . .

"Have you ordered appropriate films—something senti-mental with a religious or brotherly flavor rather than the 'Dance, Girl, Dance' variety? The National Circuit will probably send you 'Tarawa' or 'Citizen Kane' . . . so you'd better feather your yuletide nest with your own additional program—religion—sweet—music—snow, you know."

The prisoners easily fell into step with the film program, especially when the movies did not have World War II themes. They enjoyed the films, so they wanted to do everything correct-ly. Courtesy required POWs to stand at attention and salute whenever the national anthem of the United States was played, even in films. One day, before prisoners at Camp McAlester, Oklahoma, were shown the film *Dixie*, one of their interpreters requested an interview with the American compound comman-der. "Isn't it true," he asked, "that the song 'Dixie' is a sort of national anthem in your country?"

The Southern-born lieutenant replied, "Yes, sort of."

"Then, when 'Dixie' is played," reasoned the German, "we should stand at attention and salute, shouldn't we?"

"You're damned right, you should," was the loyal response of the officer.

That day, every time Bing Crosby sang the theme song of the film, the entire audience stood at attention and saluted until the last note faded away.

In addition to feature films, OWI documentaries and other propaganda films were regularly offered and used as lecture material. At many camps lectures were held that were coordi-nated with filmstrips, and religious films were also shown to POWs. Three religious films from the YMCA and eleven educa-tional filmstrips were shown and discussed at fourteen such meetings in November and December 1944 and January 1945 at Fort Bragg. Some of the topics were "Electing a President,"

"Training in Democracy," "Power from Boulder Dam," and "Our National Parks."

Unquestionably, the most convincing and damaging evidence against Hitler's regime shown to the prisoners was contained in the obviously genuine, well-produced documentaries which blended many familiar German scenes and personalities with concentration camp footage. Since the films demonstrated credibility through home-front scenes that could not be faked, the vision of huge charnel houses and slave-labor camps could hardly fail to carry conviction. The POWs, naturally, expected to be subjected to propaganda. Had the films been less convincing, they would have been easily dismissed.

Reaction to the films of concentration camps, POW camps, and Nazi atrocities against civilians in conquered lands was mixed at first. But, gradually, POWs realized that they were watching the truth. In camps around the country, the films and the accompanying booklet *Deutsche Konzentrations- und Gefangenenlager was die amerikanischen und britischen Armeen vorfanden April 1945* ("German Concentration and Prisoner-of-War Camps as the American and British Armies Found Them, April 1945") had a marked effect.

POW Josef K. and his comrades at Camp Shelby were shocked to see the films. He remembered: "We were forced to watch the movies about the concentration camps. This was the first knowledge we had of these things happening. It was hard for the Americans to believe, but we really didn't know."

A thousand men at Camp Butner voluntarily burned their German uniforms. At other camps, prisoners took up collections for the survivors of the German camps. The spokesman at Camp Blandings, Florida, added the note:

The whole company had the occasion on 10 June 1945 to convince itself through a moving picture how the German government, during the past years, has mistreated and tortured to death citizens, foreigners and prisoners of war in concentration camps and POW camps.

Voluntarily, the company decided to forward the amount of $411.00 to the German Red Cross, to be used for women, children and men, regardless of religion, who have suffered the most during the years of the German government. . . . We hope that all those criminals, regardless of class, religion, party, organization or military unit, will suffer just punishment.

Films, generally, proved to be excellent reeducation tools. Entertainment films, especially, were perfectly camouflaged lessons which were extremely popular and caught the enemy unprepared. While it is impossible to measure the effect of the film program alone, some specifics were pinpointed by the SPD. Most prisoners agreed that the average American film was better than the average German film, and the best were far superior to their German counterparts. Through films the prisoners learned of the vastness and cultural variety of the United States—rural versus urban, Northern versus Southern, industrial versus agricultural—and of its scenic splendors. Films also sold most prisoners on the American people as easygoing but clever, and on the desirability of living in America.

Other media were carefully scrutinized, too. This meant that camp publications were watched for Nazi content but, more important, that American publications entering the camps were screened. (It was usually up to the camp CO or AEO to restrict these publications.) Several of the German-language newspapers published in the United States were banned because of their National Socialist leanings or German chauvinism. *The German-American* was banned, on and off, for alleged Communist ideas. On the other hand, the *New York Staats-Zeitung*, widely distributed, was frowned upon by Nazi elements for its Allied leanings.

The New York Times was particularly popular because it

published German war communiqués along with the Allied ones. The SPD considered it so valuable that in May 1945, when the increasing scarcity of newsprint made it impossible for the *Times* to fill all the subscription requests received from POW camps, Davison attempted to obtain a special allotment of newsprint for the paper.

By the fall of 1945, SPD policy was moving away from restrictions on reading material, and the prisoners were offered a wide assortment of American publications for purchase in the canteens. Big sellers were the *Infantry Journal, Time, Life, Look, Newsweek*, the *Saturday Evening Post,* the *Times*, the *Christian Science Monitor*, the *New York Staats-Zeitung*, local newspapers, and, of course, *Der Ruf*. Prisoners could also subscribe to almost any other periodical or newspaper of interest to them.

According to Robert L. Kunzig, such an open policy was quite unique: "It was a fascinating thing from the standpoint of a nation doing something like this. Not in the sense of brainwashing, beating, controlling thought, but totally open. Read *The New York Times*. Read *Time*, or whatever it may be. Listen to the radio. Do it all."

The free expression of opinion in the American press was completely alien to the prisoners. POW Willie V. at Camp Reynolds, Pennsylvania, remarked that it was "funny·to read on one page that the Germans are steadily weakening and then turn to another page and read where some official warns that Germany is still strong!" Such freedom to speculate and disagree seemed like contradictions to him. One or the other must be lying, he thought. He was used to a press that presented only one line.

To be sure, not all the suggestions made for opening up reading material for reeducation were used. One of the early ideas thrown out by Davison, to use the wrappings of goods coming to the prisoners as a source of information, was never tried.

The only significant case of censorship of an American paper entering the camp involved the *Chicago Tribune*, which had been banned from several camps early in the war because of its obviously biased, gung-ho war coverage, which the prisoners found laughable. Apparently, this later led to a misunderstanding that nearly resulted in some very embarrassing publicity for the SPD.

At the November 1944 conference at Fort Slocum, the AEO training school, an overzealous instructor quoted some comments Colonel Davison had made at a meeting which implied he felt that the *Tribune* should not be allowed in the camps. Davison had noted that "some American newspapers are not as good as others." Reporting the problems that had occurred with prisoner reaction to *Tribune* stories, he recommended that camps promote *The New York Times* and the *Christian Science Monitor* "because they are the best liked." The instructor, in repeating the discussion, left the AEOs with the impression that the *Tribune* should be kept out of POW camps.

Two officers on their arrival to coordinate the program in the Seventh Service Command, believing they were complying with orders from the conference, sent out a directive ordering subscriptions to the *Tribune* canceled at Camp Concordia. And the new AEO at Camp Trinidad, Colorado, the same day canceled 180 orders for the paper.

There was a flurry of activity in the SPD and the service command to correct the moves before the *Tribune* got wind of it. Davison optimistically suggested to General Bryan that, should word get out, they could fall back on the fact that it was the prerogative of the camp CO to ban newspapers. He added: "The best thing to do is to keep the offense down to the lowest possible echelon. That is, to say Trinidad banned it for Trinidad—for Trinidad to say, well, there was some reason that day. Either that there were too many copies going in and they were saving newsprint, or that there was something in the edition they didn't want."

The cover-up must have worked because the *Tribune* apparently never caught on and, in fact, in September 1945 took pride in the assistance it had given to the by then declassified reeducation program. (The AEO at Concordia had prepared a digest of "suitable articles" from the *Tribune* to use as an instruction booklet.)

Allowing uncensored American reading matter into the camps, along with *Der Ruf*, had a marked effect on the content and tone of the camp papers by the fall of 1945. At Camp Maxey, Texas, the October 28, 1945, edition of *Echo*, the camp paper, showed the obvious victory of American free speech. In the lead article, the editors discussed prisoner dissatisfaction with the news that they were to be shipped to France to do reconstruction work before going home to Germany. The second article was a slam at the French for being too lenient to Nazis in their zone of occupation. The longest piece was one of a continuing series called "Our Change of Mind" in which individual prisoners discussed how repressive Nazism had been. It was a familiar example of how POWs were learning that one could disagree with authority and also openly oppose the remnants of Hitlerism without fear.

It was the same in most camps. In a publication at Fort Leonard Wood, Missouri, prisoners published information from the American zone of occupation, including a detailed article on Hermann Göring's revealed income—both salary and kickbacks. It also applauded the fact that a thousand civil servants had been fired. The editors wrote: "They will be replaced by more moral people to build up Germany in a democratic sense in the future."

Skillful use of the arts supported the other media. Not just the actual content of the specific activity but all the work that went into it was used by the AEOs as a teaching device. The popular music program was a case in point. In all the camps prisoners had formed bands, glee clubs, or large orchestras. The text *Music in America*, prepared at Fort Kearney, was distributed to all the camps. The AEOs saw to it that prisoners had enough instruments; then they began introducing music suited for "intellectual diversion."

Camp orchestras played everything from classics to jazz (which prisoners learned to appreciate listening to American radio). At Fort Devens, Massachusetts, during the winter of 1944-45 there was both a concert of nine works, which included ballet music from the opera *Rosamunde* by Franz Schubert and the Sousa march "Stars and Stripes Forever," and a comedy revue, *Laugh with Us!*, which featured the "7 Colorados" ("*die singenden* cowboys") among the dozen acts.

American music, pre-Hitler German folk songs, and, of course, music by proscribed composers, Jews, and blacks caught on in the camps. The Germans, a musically inclined people, began to readily appreciate the works of Mendelssohn and the Gershwins. They could find no danger to the Reich in their melodies.

Glee clubs and bands were the most popular cultural activities in most camps. The band at Fort Dix, New Jersey, was renowned for its dance music, entertaining prisoners and camp authorities alike (even though at dances prisoners were not allowed female dance partners). Two of the favorite numbers were "Pistol Packin' Mama" and "Mairzy Doats."

At Camp Butner, the music program was so successful that there were never enough instruments to go around. The AEO seized that opportunity to teach the POWs a bit more about tolerance for others. He wrote: "When special purchases were authorized we contacted a 'special source.' For many months the prisoners had been told of the difficulty of procuring instruments in war time, and then one day we brought Mr. Goldman in. Mr. Goldman is exactly five feet high and exudes a girth any three men would be proud of . . . and he is obviously Jewish."

Goldman, a local dealer in musical instruments, supplied all manner of instruments to the prisoners, which were paid for from canteen funds. He rapidly became a local hero and was always surrounded by friendly, appreciative Germans when he was in camp.

The AEO recorded: "After about one month of business with this good-natured Jewish merchant, they all like him. You can see it. . . . You can feel it. And the number of instruments with which to 'advertise' American music multiplies."

Similar methods were used for stimulating interest in education drama. The AEO had lists of plays—some of them provided by the SPD and the Factory and some acquired by the AEOs themselves. They helped with organizing dramatic clubs, getting material for sets and costumes, coaching the actors, and encouraging the performance of the plays on the lists. They also encouraged original playwriting (subject to censorship) among the prisoners.

In February 1945, prisoners at Camp Trinidad produced Goethe's *Iphigenie Auf Tauris*, which followed their December smash hit of Shakespeare's *Was Ihr Wollt (As You Like It)*.

There was some outside entertainment, too. Visiting troupes performed at many camps, and broadcasts of patriotic radio programs were piped in over camp public-address systems.

There was no objection to prisoners owning radios. In fact, one job of the AEOs was to determine the prisoners' listening habits and to try to get them to listen to the "right" programs —to American news reports and music. (The sets were checked periodically to assure that they did not have sending capacity.)

Another form of visual education was exhibitions put on by the prisoners themselves. These displays could be about anything from architectural concepts to beekeeping. (At several camps prisoners kept hives.) AEOs were directed to select a director of exhibits from among the friendly prisoners and to encourage "displays and posters without politico-social significance to begin with. Follow through with posters and displays having both artistic and educational value." And, above all, to "emphasize basic moral and ethical precepts—art with a social purpose—to create conflict and stimulate thought."

Thomas Mann's publisher, Bermann-Fischer Verlag, helped stimulate other cultural expression by the prisoners. Besides its work with the *Neue Welt* books, the publishing house, based in Stockholm during the war, sponsored a literary contest. Several hundred original novels were submitted. First prize went to Walter Kolbenhoff, a previously published novelist. His winning novel, *Von Unsern Fleisch und Blut* ("From Our Flesh and Blood"), gained him three thousand marks in prize money and was published by Bermann-Fischer and the Peter Suhrkamp Verlag (Berlin) in 1946.

Many reeducation projects were suggested to the American authorities by sincere anti-Nazis or converted Germans who used their leisure time to mull over their lessons. Usually they urged the start of a reeducation program unaware that they were already taking part in one. Ernst D. wrote from Camp Hearne: "Would it not be a noble task for American universities, professors, representatives of public life, to teach German prisoners how to look at history, politics, etc., with the eyes of a free man, to illustrate to them the achievements of democracy in America?" The SPD could not have said it better. Prisoners who hoped to work in such a program included a large number of Catholic chaplains.

Many men volunteered to write letters or record speeches to be given in Germany so their relatives and friends would not believe, as Claus von W. said, "that we have forgotten we are Germans, just because we look upon Nazis as our enemies."

In the fall of 1945, there was a storm of letters from prisoners volunteering to join the American Army to fight for, in the words of POW Erich F., the "annihilation of Nazism, conclusion of the war and eventual reconstruction of a way of life in some country, in case the U.S.A. rejects immigrants."

The Nazis had frowned on existing religions, so a very important aspect of the Intellectual Diversion Program was to return the men to Christian practices. Reading the Bible had gone out of favor along with churchgoing as Nazism became a religion as well as a political ideology. Nazi camp leaders ridiculed men who attended church services and often desecrated the chapels. Only a few men in each camp braved the verbal abuse to follow their consciences.

To deal with this problem, the SPD had obtained a chaplain, Captain John Dvorovy, but the shortage of German Army chaplains was a critical impasse for him. Many camps did not have one, and the POWs were wary of getting too friendly with the American chaplain. Primarily they feared repercussions from the Nazis, but they also had a natural distrust of the "enemy."

The most successful method for winning the men back to religious attendance was to manipulate them into opting for it themselves. With this in mind, the AEO would call the company leaders together and have them vote on whether they wanted an official chapel and chaplain. Only the most convinced Nazis were willing to risk their immortal souls by voting in the negative, so chapels were usually approved. Once that was decided, there remained the question of whether they should be Catholic or Protestant.

To resolve it, the members of each POW company had to be polled. This meant that Nazi leaders had to at least allow religious preferences to be discussed, and free discussion is the surest way to beat repressive systems like Nazism. Many previously unwilling to declare themselves saw this as an opportunity to return to God.

Religious literature available in several languages flowed into the camps. Everything from Bibles to rosary beads and religious medals was passed to the men through the chaplains.

The AEO saw to it that no other activities conflicted with religious classes or services; and, of course, public-address systems were silent Sunday mornings.

The program was an enormous success. Most camps eventually had two chapels—one for each group. Many camps built religious shrines. And, naturally, the Christian principle of "love thy neighbor" blended perfectly with the overall plan for "intellectual diversion."

The Intellectual Diversion Program encompassed recreational activities, too. Equipment was provided for both German and American games, with the emphasis swinging toward the latter as the program developed. Even at the most Nazi-oriented segregation camps, all-American sports like baseball and horseshoe-pitching became popular pastimes. Competitive matches from checkers to soccer were encouraged to improve the morale and adaptation of the prisoners.

Gradually, the POWSPD decided to attempt another kind of American competition—political elections. Many AEOs had requested permission to try putting the classroom lessons to work within their camps. Finally, a few were permitted to try it. The most successful was at Camp Mackall, North Carolina.

The prisoners formed four political parties—the Democratic Party, the Christian Democratic Party, the Party of the United Nations, and the Social Democratic Party—and nominated candidates for camp spokesman and company leader. Elections were held on September 23, 1945. The race was a close one, with the Democratic and Christian Democratic Party candidates finishing a few votes apart. The Democrats won the camp spokesman seat by one vote, and the Christian Democrats took the company leadership by four.

The party chiefs sent an affidavit to the Provost Marshal General's Office asking that they be declared a "democratic camp" because of the successful completion of their elections.

Many within the SPD were not pleased with the decision to allow the elections. They felt it was just an exercise by the AEOs to show how personally successful they had been. SPD members joked that the 97 percent who voted in one of the camps just indicated how forced the activity was. They wrote sarcastically: "It may be assumed that no stone was left unthrown in an effort to browbeat the prisoners into this amazing demonstration of democracy in action. No such majority, it might be well to point out, has ever been recorded in an American election."*

Whatever the true motivation behind holding the elections, the existing records indicate that the prisoners campaigned with gusto and quite possibly learned a little something about the process of free elections.

Several times the secrecy of the Intellectual Diversion Program was nearly uncovered by overzealous American anti-Nazis. Each time, the publicity given to the unaware do-gooders left the War Department scurrying around to cover its tracks.

The first was Gerhart Seger, editor of the *Neue Volkszeitung* in New York and a concentration camp escapee. Just as the reeducation program was beginning, he received a great deal of coverage in the press by forming a committee to promote the reeducation of German POWs and publicly demanding a joint session of the Senate and House Military Affairs committees to discuss his proposals. By midsummer 1944, the situation was getting touchy. The POWSPD was going full steam, and Seger was getting more publicity as he repeatedly tried and failed to see General George C. Marshall.

His Marshall campaign finally got the War Department moving, and General Bryan was ordered to get Seger out of the picture. They met in August 1944. Bryan did not tell Seger of the existing program, but he did inform him that a plan would be undertaken by the War Department. He also assured Seger that no civilians would be allowed to participate in the program and that it would not be publicized, since the prisoners read the newspapers. Bryan must have been very convincing because

---

*It is interesting to note here that according to Wolfgang Wagner, editor of the *Hannoversche Allgemeine Zeitung*, in an editorial in *The Washington Post*, August 12, 1976, 91 percent of the eligible Germans voted in the national elections in West Germany in 1972. Perhaps their brush with Nazism taught them to take the right to vote more seriously than Americans do.

Seger backed down. Although POW camp papers did reprint many stories about Seger's proposal, it did not seem to hurt the fledgling program badly.

Around the same period, William L. Shirer, who had nearly blown a hole in the intelligence program with an earlier story, began campaigning on a note similar to Seger's. In newspaper articles Shirer urged the reeducation of prisoners: "I may be wrong, but in as much as the President says we are going to stamp out Nazism in Germany and the Vice President says we are going to re-educate the master race, I've been wondering whether it wouldn't be possible and perhaps even desirable to begin right here at home with the specimens we have in the German prisoner of war camps."

His arguments were persuasive, suggesting that unless we reeducated these men they would someday start World War III. He claimed to have discussed the idea with army officials and to have been rebuffed many times.

In a burst of oversimplification and naiveté, Shirer added: "Anyone with any knowledge of German and the Nazi mentality knows that this Nazi terror against those German prisoners who no longer wish to conform to Hitler's teachings could be stopped overnight by simply letting the Gestapo-minded prisoners know that this democracy simply will not tolerate such nonsense."

Coming when they did, Shirer's articles upset program planners, as any information putting the prisoners on their guard might, but his attack on the army's refusal to reeducate could only lead the suspicious POW to assume he was safe. Shirer's view of the army's shortsightedness must have caused a large sigh of relief at the POWSPD.

In April 1945, less than a month before V-E Day and five months after the arrival of the AEOs at the camps, Representative Richard F. Harless of Arizona toured Camp Papago Park. The reeducation program was still classified, and one can only guess how much Harless saw of it, but he received a lot of personal publicity by loudly demanding in Congress that German prisoners be "thoroughly indoctrinated into the workings of democracy." As the precedent for such a program, he cited an alleged Russian program of training anti-Nazis in their POW camps to help them control Germany and spread communism. The United States, he erroneously argued, "has not done a single thing to educate German prisoners in the American way of life."

Reports of a Russian program had been circulating for months. Contrary to the information now known about the Russian camps, where thousands of Germans died from freezing and starvation, reports in American periodicals in the fall and winter of 1944-45 alleged excellent treatment by the Russians in order to convert the men to anti-Nazi, pro-Communist politics.

Although no Allied observers were ever allowed to see the program in action, many writers believed the Soviet story and published articles lauding their work. Henry C. Cassidy wrote in *The Atlantic Monthly* that "the Russians have felt free to experiment. Their finished product—education made available to the prisoner and propaganda tools put in his hands—deserves a place in the future military machine of any country." Allegedly, the Russians had established a Free German National Committee and had begun reeducating POWs immediately after their capture. Several high-ranking German generals captured at Stalingrad were reported to be supporting the project. Many of the most respected American magazines (read by prisoners) published these stories as part of a public campaign advocating prisoner reeducation. The army knew the Germans must have seen them.

Several other do-gooders wrote to the War Department, the secretary of war, and even Secretary of the Interior Harold Ickes. Offers ranged from mass reeducation plans to encounter sessions with a minister or professor for groups of twelve. The writers received pleasant, noncommittal replies.

The closest call the program's secrecy ever had occurred in Waco, Texas. In February 1945, an officer from Camp Mexia made a speech to the Waco Kiwanis Club. The next day the *Waco*

News Tribune headlined "Courses in American Life Taught POWs." It went on to explain that "this orientation program is encouraged with a view toward influencing the attitudes of POWs toward the United States after their repatriation to Germany following the war."

The Eighth Service Command immediately ordered the story killed before it could be released by the wire services, but they never picked it up, anyway. In a comment to the Waco paper, the army called the story "fanciful."

It may have been fanciful in Texas, but next door in Florence, Arizona, internees at a previously pro-Nazi POW camp would shortly send a heartfelt letter of condolence to the army on the death of President Franklin D. Roosevelt. They followed it with a long letter that they wanted transmitted to the German people calling for them to lay down their arms. "Root out the last Werewolf nest," they wrote, "and prepare the path for a true democratic-republican Germany." And prisoners at Camp Indianola, Nebraska, prepared a statement condemning the horrors of Nazi concentration camps and the "hopelessness, fear, hunger and sickness" left as Hitler's legacy.

On May 28, 1945, twenty days after V-E Day, the existence of a reorientation program for German POWs was announced to the public. Declassification had been argued within the War Department since early April. The anti-release faction argued that there was a vast difference between prisoners suspecting a program existed and their being told outright. The faction feared, as Otto Englander wrote, that the "moment they are sure of being 'victimized' their minds will be impervious to any new ideas." Howard Mumford Jones felt that declassification would open the program to assaults from do-gooders and, if worded without care, could leave our Allies with the very uncomfortable feeling that we were Americanizing the POWs.

Considering that the Canadians were using the United States, the richest, largest, and most successful of the democratic countries, as the model in most of their reeducation work, the latter argument was a bit weak. Only the Russians might, predictably, accuse us of making the program "too American."

Pro-declassification officers argued that the unconditional surrender of Germany "largely eliminated the reasons for declassification." They agreed with General Bryan that disclosure of the program would lead to greater progress. Bryan also maintained that since many newspaper and radio people had already found out about the program, it would be impossible to keep it secret much longer, anyway.

A seven-page statement was released under Bryan's name on May 28. In it he explained: "We are taking some 350,000 German prisoners of war—men meandering in a morass of myths—and conducting a well-calculated, thorough and pointed program of exposition." A general description of the content and methods of the program was included in the report. Bryan concluded that it might not be the only way to conduct such a program, but it "is a good way though—the results show that. It is an American way."

Most of the press seemed to have missed the significance of Bryan's announcement. While national newspapers like *The New York Times* and the *Chicago Tribune* ran periodic articles from that point on, depicting the success of the program, popular periodicals, which had for months been harping on the issue of whether the United States "pampered" POWs, failed to pick up on it or ran one story casually mentioning it.

One week after declassification, *Collier's* published yet another editorial on the "pampering" question. It lauded the American treatment of POWs as one factor contributing to the mass German surrenders in Europe, yet failed to even acknowledge that part of our good treatment emanated from our desire to reeducate.

American magazine, which, like *Collier's*, had been following POW murders and work programs, published another article in July 1945. The writer somehow managed to spend several days at a POW camp seeing only the spinach harvest, completely ignoring the reeducation program. Either the press of 1945 was not very alert, or it had utterly failed to recognize the significance of what the army had just admitted it was doing.

One of the most spectacular demonstrations of the success of reeducation was put together at Fort Benning, Georgia, in October 1945. At a special projects conference for AEOs, two prisoners from the base and each of thirteen branch camps showed the results of the amazing program they had been involved in. The three-day event included classes, plays, and lectures by democratized prisoners.

In a special edition of their publication *Wille und Weg* ("Will and Way"), entitled *UND DENNOCH, WIR MACHEN WEI-TER* ("Nevertheless, We Will Carry On"), the prisoners published the voluntary pledge they had signed October 25. It began:

> We accept the Re-education Program "American Government and Democracy" to develop a new basis for the spiritual reformation of the Germans and the reconstruction of the German Nation. Since the inner collapse of our people was at last due to a systematic seclusion from the word and ideas of Western Democracy, we saw our first task . . . to create for ourselves . . . a glance into the construction and life of a state, which from the beginning of its history had only one desire, the freedom of its citizens, the welfare of their life, and the peace of all those who lived within its borders.

The booklet also contained fourteen pages of charts explaining the Bill of Rights, the Constitution, Federalism, separation of powers, the growth of democracy in colonial America, and other areas of democratic triumph. The lessons they had received obviously included an even better picture of the inseparable bond between our history, capitalist economics, and civics than American schoolchildren receive.

In all, the forty-four-page special edition of *Wille und Weg* was a very professional and quite remarkable educational tool in itself.

The success of the camp reeducation programs is very difficult to assess. There were so many camps, each with a different AEO and a slightly different program. The AEO at Camp Concordia had a very realistic attitude when he wrote: "The prisoners of war leaving this camp cannot be considered as having suddenly become thoroughly democratic as a whole, but they have been given, and have seized the opportunity, to study America as a nation and as a functioning democracy, and under reasonably equitable circumstances this study will bear fruit."

6 Special Projects

IN EARLY 1945, the army realized that in order to efficiently administer the U.S. zone of occupation, it would need trained, trustworthy Germans. A conference was called at the Factory, with army representatives and twelve especially highly regarded prisoners present. They recommended the establishment of schools to train administrative and police personnel from among the POWs.

An experiment in administrative training was conducted at Fort Kearney for two months—May to July—to test the idea. Sixty of the prisoners were divided into two groups to study English, history, civics, and military government. Graduation exercises were held July 6.

The Kearney experiment was a huge success. Besides proving that the prisoners quartered there were extremely able, it provided three important results. First, it proved that such a school could produce graduates with a level of achievement to do the job. Second, it created the first group of prisoners actually qualified to work in military government. And third, it revealed important problems that would be encountered in developing the project on a larger scale—particularly the need for a large, highly skilled faculty and the limitations a sixty-day period would impose.

Ultimately, three schools were established. In the United States, the administrative school at Fort Getty was approved on May 19, 1945, and the police school at Fort Wetherill on June 2. Both sites were on Narragansett Bay, across from Fort Kearney. A third school, at Querqueville, France, was established during the summer of 1945 to train desirable prisoners still held in Europe in administrative work.

To clear men for Forts Getty and Wetherill, screening teams were created which, in addition to American personnel, included six men from the Factory. The prisoners went through two series of tests, first in their own camps, then in groups at Fort Devens, Massachusetts. Of 17,883 men screened, only 816 were accepted for the administrative school and 2,895 for the police school.

The tests, under the supervision of a German, Dr. Henry W. Ehrmann, who had fled Hitler and ultimately become a civilian expert for the POWSPD and an instructor at Getty, Wetherill, and Fort Eustis, had a threefold purpose. Besides providing the obvious information on the general knowledge, intelligence level, and political attitudes of the prisoners, they were a check on the prisoners' own statements about their education and political beliefs, they helped to determine whether the man really was a suitable candidate for the schools and for which school he was best qualified, and, lastly, the answers given in the written tests could later be used in conversations to help judge the honesty and intelligence of the man.

Although the PMGO, with the Supreme Headquarters Allied Expeditionary Force in France, had requested that the POWs selected for special training be natives of communities to be within the American zone of occupation, this was never done. It would have been far too difficult to find an adequate number of men with this as a prime criterion of selection. Other back-ground—politics, knowledge of English—took precedence.

It is doubtful that any real Nazis could have slipped through the extensive testing. As Kunzig remarked: "If someone in the early stages at Kearney and Getty had not been a pretty sincere anti-Nazi, boy, that was found out—by the others! A pretty cold-blooded operation! He'd be out."

Of the men selected, 43 percent were university graduates: engineers, teachers, or others; 25 percent were businessmen or other kinds of white-collar workers; and 10 percent had been German civil servants. Clearly, this was a group with strong capabilities.

The spirit at Getty was every bit as cohesive as at Kearney, in large part due to the caliber of the faculty. Dr. William G. Moulton, who was assistant director of the language department, commented: "We had Howard Mumford Jones, T. V. Smith, Haxey Smith [Dr. Henry Lee Smith, Jr.], Alpheus Smith, Henry Ehrmann—Haxey was a major, I was a captain. Ed Kennard [Dr. Edward Kennard] was a sergeant. He was every bit as capable as we were, and he was treated accordingly. This made a big impression on the prisoners. How Edward Davison got this group of people together, I'll never know, but this was some group."

In addition to the 58 American officer faculty members and 115 enlisted men, a number of Germans were recruited from the group at Kearney. Many of the German Getty graduates, selected later to teach their fellow prisoners, returned to the United States after the war to serve at the Foreign Service Institute's School of Language and Linguistics with Henry Lee Smith.

Many of the Americans came from Kearney, too, moving across the bay to Getty but still teaching at Kearney and also at Wetherill, and keeping close ties with personnel there. Conse-quently, the camaraderie and brotherhood of Kearney was trans-ported to Getty, a unique example to the students. At the core of this group were the three Smiths, Jones, Moulton, and Commander Edwin Casady, the navy's contribution to the program. They never failed to find humor in everything to keep spirits high. As Kunzig wrote to Davison and Schoenstedt from Kearney while the latter were setting up the Querqueville school: "Getty even has buildings named for you. . . . Hank Smith is planning on naming an attractive latrine in Lerch Hall for me."

They were also extremely dedicated to the goals and the students in the program. Kunzig noted: "I've been trying to figure out why this was so thrilling to us. Part of it was that we were getting wonderful responses from each other and from a lot of the prisoners. And again and again that's the picture. It wasn't so much what they'd learned, what we'd taught them, but the general spirit of the place."

Dr. Walter Hallstein, the most prominent of all the Getty graduates, who was to become president of the European Economic Community in the 1960s, echoed those sentiments. He wrote: "The atmosphere in the stalag between the inmates, the teachers and the staff was terrific. . . . The selection of the faculty and the methods they used to present the material made it very successful."

Today, those who were part of the American staff hate to have the word *reeducation* applied to what was done at Forts Kearney and Getty. Perhaps the tone of the German history lectures at Getty was closer to the point. The classes were taught by Dr. Ehrmann, who wanted to remind the men of the direction in which German history might have gone. He did not have to convince them that in the 1930s Germany had headed down the wrong path; what he had to show them was the way it could have gone instead.

Moulton's reaction was: "I hate the word *reeducation*. I remember when one of our PWs spoke before a *Herald Tribune Forum* [on October 30, 1945]. He started off by saying that when he arrived at Getty and heard the word *reeducation* he thought, 'My God, I don't need to be reeducated.' This was a real blow."

In his speech, POW Wolf Dieter Zander, who had risen from prisoner to faculty assistant in the American history section at Forts Getty and Wetherill, described his and his fellow-prisoners' feelings of bitterness at being told they had to be reoriented. Many at Getty, he said, had spent years in concentration camps in Germany for their political beliefs. They resented having their philosophy so questioned. But the attitude of the faculty and the mutual desire to reform Germany helped them overcome this bitterness. He recounted: "Within a few days, however, we lost our feelings of insecurity. And the cynics presently lost their following. . . . In discussions and talks our hosts showed again and again their peculiar mixture of reason and unaffected, contagious optimism. Their self-criticism on the one hand, and their belief in the sanctity of the individual on the other, helped us to recover values long buried in our past."

Many of the prisoners who were students at Getty, Kearney, and Querqueville did not need reeducation in the strict sense. What they needed was a push in the right direction to conform with occupation policy and the postwar world.

On October 20, 1945, Dr. Hallstein gave the graduation address on behalf of his classmates. In a touching oration he reflected on what the course had meant to them:

> All this means more to us than a renewed knowledge, it means to us a living experience—this is a success that can't be achieved by ever so refined a method.
>
> We owe it rather to the fact that we have found the right teachers. . . . In no province of social relations, neither in that of education . . . can there be any effect from man to man if one is not to devote to it a part of his very self. . . . Therefore, this is our happiest experience: that, here, in an atmosphere of spontaneous humanity and naturalness we have found a spiritual contact with men with whom we

shall be connected forever by a feeling of sincere and high respect, often fond affection.

One social lesson that was learned quickly through the attitude of the Americans was the end of elitism inbred in the German Army. In the beginning, the students at Getty noticed that some discussions were presided over by officers, some by enlisted men, and some by civilians. The status-conscious Germans initially believed that those in groups led by a high-ranking officer would get the most influencial jobs in the military government and the rest of the jobs would be handed out in a corresponding manner right down the line.

This was disproved by the casualness by which the POWSPD officers and teachers regarded their rank. Many of the officer-teachers had no military training at all—Dr. Moulton, for instance, who was given a captaincy, was told by General Bryan: "For God's sake, learn how to salute." There was no concern for military rank among them or in their dealings with the prisoners. One prisoner, after a private meeting with Moulton, contemplated the difference between the Americans and the German military elite. "You know," he said, "this is the first time I've ever talked to a captain."

The courses at Fort Getty were geared to a high level of competency by the commanding officer, Lieutenant Colonel Alpheus Smith. Dr. Smith established one principle upon which an "affirmative climate for action" was set for students and faculty alike. His standard assumed that everyone was giving his best to the project and would do so when treated as if he were expected to do so.

The carefully planned and tested course schedule at Getty concentrated on four topic areas: military government, English, American history, and German history.

The military government courses were taught by Major Burnham Dell, once described as a "gentle soldier and sagacious man," who taught the students every trick of the trade that they might conceivably need in working with the occupation government. The texts were *Handbook of Military Government in Germany, Civil Affairs Handbook* (about civil affairs in Germany), and *Civil Affairs Guide*.

The students were also required to read official material about the situation in Germany after V-E Day. They pored over the Military Government Weekly Field Reports—SHAEF and the Monthly Reports of the Military Governor—American Zone. This was more than class work for them, it was their first real look at the situation at home.

Dell spoke in English while a "monitor" (interpreter) translated a summary into German. The monitors led weekly review sessions covering all of the subject matter.

Dr. Ehrmann chaired the courses in German history, which were taught on a daily basis. His aim was to give the students a new set of references for past history in Germany and to dispel the propagandized history taught in the schools of Nazi Germany. Many prisoners believed that democratization was incompatible with historic patterns of German behavior. Ehrmann's job was to dissuade them.

Ehrmann and four German-speaking instructors (and two POW assistants) began their lessons with the Treaty of Westphalia, since the entrance exams had shown a striking lack of knowledge of basic German history even among college-educated men. Fifty percent of the candidates for Getty were unable to identify either the Paulskirche in Frankfurt, symbol of the Revolution of 1848, or Rudolf Virchow, Bismarck's liberal antagonist. Fifty percent could neither identify Carl Schurz nor name a single Social Democratic leader of the pre-World War I era. Even more (57 percent) did not recognize the name of Hugo Preuss, father of the Weimar Constitution.

In the younger men these failings were recognized as a result of the Nazi system of education in the 1930s. In the older men it seemed to prove the widely held theory that the lower middle classes in Germany were ignorant of history and politics—an important factor in Hitler's rise to power.

To fill in these gaps in the knowledge of the students at Getty and at the police school at Wetherill, as much information as possible was provided about the historic manifestations of the German people's desire and ability to fight for freedom. Local government, the intellectual traditions of Germany's classic period, the Revolution of 1848, the opposition under Bismarck and Wilhelm II, and the German Youth Movement were all investigated and their democratic leanings capitalized upon.

As a balance, the inner weakness of these movements was openly admitted and analyzed. Particular emphasis was placed on the escapist tendencies of many leaders of the movements which led them to metaphysics instead of political realities.

American history and the principles of democracy were taught by Dr. T. V. Smith and staff. Howard Mumford Jones, director of education for the reeducation program, felt communications problems involved in teaching this course were particularly severe. He wrote:

An American who wants to explain democracy to the Germans sometimes finds himself a little baffled. He can, of course, begin with the Declaration of Independence and go on to the Constitution and the Gettysburg Address. He can do this in English or he can do it in German. Somehow it seems better, whenever possible, to use the English texts; the Constitution in German translation suffers a weird sea-change into political metaphysics. . . . But if he sticks to English texts, he finds he has to explain an eighteenth-century or biblical vocabulary to readers of limited English.

If he then turns to some of the handbooks on citizenship published by the Government or by some of the admirable agencies that try to help the newcomer, he finds these are not designed for his needs. Most of the handbooks are meant for adults of meager literacy, and some of the writing is . . . infantile. Germans have been accused of many faults, but illiteracy has never been one of them.

The plan was to teach history in such a way as to aid the Germans in developing an objective view of their immediate past and to encourage democratic solutions to the resulting problems. A fine mixture of politics, sociology, philosophy, and literature was taught in an effort to "dazzle" the prisoners with the magnificence of the democratic way of life.

Democracy was presented as a system which has been successful in fulfilling man's aspirations for a free and happy life, and as a real challenge to the German people.

The faculty of four officers and four to six group leaders used the Nevins and Commager *Pocket History of the United States*, an OWI booklet called *An American Handbook*, and three pamphlets written by Jones and translated at the Factory.

After his lectures, T. V. Smith would meet with a dozen of the most linguistically and academically advanced to discuss problem areas further. After the lecture on the Civil War, the session was particularly animated. His strategy was to show that all countries had their failures—Germany in the failure of democracy in Weimar, and the United States—most obviously—in "trying to solve our worst moral problem by means of force." It was, the group concluded, the elimination by extremists on both sides of a middle ground on which to compromise that led to these failures.

Discussions of the Civil War inevitably led to the most pointed and threatening questions in the American history program. Slavery, racism, racial segregation, and the irony of trying to teach freedom behind barbed wire were always mentioned. The prisoners pointed out the huge discrepancies between Anglo-American practice and pretense in each of these sessions. The subject bewildered them in its complexity.

The favorite topic at Getty, Wetherill, and virtually every camp where there was a reeducation program was that of American black people. Most instructors found it extremely difficult to deal with. At Getty and Wetherill it was handled by T. V. Smith, a native Southerner, who found it easier to handle than his Northern colleagues. He said: "I was content (1) to point to its history, (2) to parade the progress that the Negroes have made since slavery, and (3) to ask for suggestions from them as to how we Americans can move faster and more securely in solving our major 'minority problems.' There was never any pretense on my part that 'democracy' is not fascism to our Negroes in certain sections and at certain times."

Reading the *Congressional Record* was encouraged. Some felt it would help the prisoners develop a better understanding of how Congress and the democratic system worked. Many prisoners were having difficulty conceiving the rule of the majority, since it was not an absolute—majorities changed with issues.

The history courses presented a clear, well-informed, critical analysis of the problems likely to be confronted in Germany. Both history curricula were followed with rapt attention by the students. Even those who had previous knowledge of the topics found food for thought in the content of each class. But the same worries kept reappearing in discussions and private talks. One was that they were a relatively small group to fight great odds in Germany. Couldn't the Americans train several million men this way?

Secondly, those who had been teachers and wanted to pursue that profession after the war pleaded for courses in the problems of education incorporated in either a German or an American history class. The system of free education for all was, of course, mentioned as a benefit of democracy, but the kind of detail needed by future educators was always lacking.

English was, in some ways, the most important subject the men studied. Without the language they would have no chance of a job with the military government. And without English the other courses of study were more difficult. The talented head of the language program was Dr. Henry Lee Smith, Jr. He was assisted in planning and instructor training by Dr. William G. Moulton, Dr. Edward Kennard, and a staff of thirty to forty instructors, making it the largest department.

According to Dr. Hallstein, of all the classes he took at Getty, English was the one that most benefited him. He wrote: "Personally to me the English language, which was in the best of hands, helped me greatly since my English at that time was very primitive.

"At that time I did not know that soon I would profit from my knowledge of English in dealing, as a high state government official, with American government people and friends."

Language instruction was geared toward a dual goal: teaching the language, and in a manner that would contribute to the larger objective of teaching democratic life.

The method used to teach English was the same one used to teach American soldiers German. The text, published by the army at the request of Henry Smith, was *Englisch wie man's spricht*. It was referred to as "reverse German," since it followed the pattern already used in the army's basic language manuals.

In order to accomplish the plan's purposes, the language setup was rather complicated. Students were divided into groups starting at three different levels and taught at two different rates of speed. The schedule was tightly organized and watched by the supervisors, partially because of the inexperience of the instructors, many of whom knew no German. The schedule also made it possible to change instructors or cover an absence and not miss or repeat any material.

Things ran so well that Moulton could stand outside a classroom with a visiting VIP and explain that the men were on page 153 "and then have the pleasure of watching his reaction when we walked in and found that they actually *were* in the middle of page 153." It was an efficient teaching method that also won plaudits from the military hierarchy.

The initial wide range of language skills caused immense

problems. Students ranged all the way from complete ignorance of English to complete fluency—including one who had been an exchange student in the United States and lived for some time in England, one who was married to an American, and one who had grown up in Canada.

To deal with this variation, the men were divided into five levels, designated A to E. The A and B levels were too fluent to learn much from the manual, so their classes were specially planned. Their first hour of the day was a meeting with either Dr. Smith or Dr. Moulton for practice in speaking. Smith specialized in improving phonetics, and Moulton worked on eliminating German speech patterns. During a second hour each day, the students would attend a seminar with a visiting speaker—the speakers included politicians, college professors, and army officers. They discussed politics, democratic principles, literature, and a variety of other subjects. One of their favorites was a discussion with a corporal from New Jersey whose topic was "Why I like Mayor Hague."

The C, D, and E language groups were divided into smaller groups of eight to ten for drill in English. They spent four hours each morning alternately drilling, studying, drilling, and studying.

The emphasis in classes was on spoken English. A student who had passed the course might still be unable to read or write English well, but he could carry on a fairly complicated conversation with ease.

At Fort Wetherill, the men had to be handled with great care. Since they were to become police, it was decided they should be more carefully screened then entrants to Kearney or Getty had been. Hence, upon arrival at Wetherill, each took a polygraph test.

Besides the army experts and interpreters from the Factory, crime fighters from around the country were obtained to supervise these tests. The experts represented the police departments of Indianapolis, Cleveland, Detroit, and Chicago, the attorney general of North Dakota, and Northwestern University's Crime Detection Laboratory.

Prior to the test, which was an individual examination, the prisoner was read this preamble:

> Because of the necessity of rebuilding and reorganizing your country in the best and quickest manner, we have deemed it important that the most reliable Germans assist. . . . You have been chosen as reliable, friendly individuals to assist us and your people. However . . . we have found some Germans, thought to be reliable, were in reality planning to interfere with our reconstruction program. For your own protection they had to be eliminated, for if one unreliable man goes to Germany as a trusted friend our and your program may be set back a long time. . . . For this reason we are to subject you to a "lie-detector" test to be sure your voiced intentions are genuine.

The preamble went on to encourage them to tell the truth, to answer all the questions, and it also explained what a lie-detector was and how it was used in American law enforcement.

In a routine elimination test, each man was asked twenty-one questions. They ranged from "Were you ever a member of the Nazi Party?" to "Do you advocate Communism for Germany?"

Problems arose because the men were allowed to start classes while awaiting the results of their polygraphs. If they were subsequently rejected for any reason (the most common was poor classwork), they assumed they had failed the polygraph test. There were vociferous complaints from many of those who had been rejected, avowing their lifelong anti-Nazism in an effort to be returned to Wetherill.

While a number were rejected because they had cooperated with the Nazi regime, at least as many failed for having Communist leanings. Many saw Wetherill as a chance for a fast ticket home and showed little enthusiasm for courses or for police careers. They, too, were weeded out.

German history, American history, English, and military government were also taught at Wetherill but on a considerably shortened schedule since the emphasis was on police training. In language instruction, for example, it was said that the "results were considerably less than half as good" because of the lack of time and courses.

While many of the instructors were the same as at Getty, few were actually stationed there. They commuted from Getty by car or ferry. Hence, despite the efforts of the CO, Major K. K. Kolster, and his staff, the rapport that existed at the other camps was never quite repeated.

Instructional emphasis at Wetherell was on the police in a democracy. Eleven officers and one civilian expert tried to instill in their pupils an understanding of the organization and operation of the police in a democratic state. Bringing this down to the local level, they also taught the policeman's role in a democratic community. The New York City Police Department was the model system used for teaching techniques and skills of the trade. (In occupied Germany, many communities also imitated New York's Finest in establishing postwar police.)

Every subject was taught with an eye toward the policeman's viewpoint. The lecture on the Bill of Rights, for example, was supplemented by a detailed discussion of the limitations on the police and the military in a democracy. The limitations on search warrants, the right of habeas corpus, the rights of the accused, the right of citizens to bear arms and their right to sue the police were covered in greater detail than the other guaranteed rights. The Nazi image of police had to be permanently erased.

Eventually, 1,166 men were graduated from Forts Getty and Wetherill. The army praised the two programs as proof that "democracy can be 'absorbed' through exposure." Perhaps, but there was a lot of hard work involved, too.

The most serious problem encountered by the POWSPD at Getty and Wetherill was that of finding new instructors. All the subject sections complained about the inadequate number of teachers. The language program, in particular, had "a bare minimum number of qualified men," the result of a snafu within the War Department. After approving and encouraging the program, certain brass found many ways to hinder it, including holding back on staff approvals for a myriad of reasons.

Teaching at these special camps was a unique experience, and each new instructor had to be specially oriented to his new assignment. He was not given any formal training for the first week or two. Instead, he was handed over to one of the head supervisors, who described the general setup to him and saw that he sat in on classes and briefings, observing experienced instructors in action.

Once he was familiar with the work, he was put in charge of a class—under the watchful eye of a supervisor. After he had become fully acquainted with the situation, he was given his first orientation lectures—his only formal training.

Henry Smith set a particularly impressive example for the novices. He gave the first lecture to the new language instructors, and Moulton gave the remaining four. With little preparation except what was in his heart, he could bring even his colleague Moulton near tears with emotional fervor. Moulton recalled: "I went in there and sat in the back. He spoke for forty minutes and at the end I was practically on my knees thanking the Lord that I was in this place at this time doing the most important thing in the world there was to do."

Since the success of the reorientation program depended so strongly on the personalities and energy of the men doing the teaching, Smith's type of introduction was necessary and highly effective.

In attempting to assess how well they were doing at Getty and Wetherill, the POWSPD tried two tests. First, they brought in a noted New York psychiatrist in November 1945 to evaluate the denazification achievements. Second, they prepared a report the next month with a committee of neuropsychiatrists which compared attitudes at Getty with those at the POW camp at Halloran General Hospital on Staten Island, New York.

The psychiatrist, Dr. Richard M. Brickner, author of *Is Germany Incurable?*, who did not believe Germans could be denazified, responded with pleased surprise after his interview with five of the prisoners. He wrote:

> Seeing the team, of such rare and devoted people, in action, was an impressive lesson. . . . You people have found out how to do it.
>
> . . . It was an impressive sight to see that young lieutenant sitting on a table not pretending to be the world's greatest authority on American history, talking it over from an overtly visible outline and laughing with the Germans. It was also a joy to see German PWs laughing and without tension or fear. . . .
>
> [Subject] (a) seems to show everything the most unthinking Germans show. But with one difference . . . he prized what he had learned about the difference between debate and discussion; in a discussion you can compromise. The impression it made on him gave me the first inkling I have had that even downright, regular, typical Germans can be impressed. . . .
>
> (b) is just a beautiful character. . . . If he can't be trusted, I would say we might as well give up. . . .
>
> (c) strikes me as more like an Irishman than a German and I have no question in my mind about him.

He was equally impressed with the other two, if less colorful in his language.

The report prepared by a committee the next month was much more complex. Five hundred men at Halloran were given three tests of political and social attitudes, including a group Rorschach test. The men were a mixture of those who had participated in the regular reeducation program at the camp. Known Nazis and anti-Nazis were included in the group. Their results were compared with the results of the same series at Getty. The men there included the POW assistants, the current classes at Getty and Wetherill, and the POW maintenance company (who serviced the camp and were of a slightly less favorable background than the students). All four groups, 101 men, were believed to be safe democrats, the difference being merely educational training.

The results showed that 92 percent of the Getty prisoners had fairly good democratic attitudes, compared with 24 percent at Halloran. Seventy-nine percent at Getty were judged to be "good risks," as opposed to 5 percent at Halloran. Surprisingly, the men from Wetherill scored on a par with the students at Getty—74 percent scored over eighty points, while 77 percent from Getty did so, also. The POW assistants were in a class by themselves, with nearly all scoring close to perfect in all categories. Even in the less-trained service company, half scored more than 80 percent on the attitude scale.

In consistency as well as in total score, the Getty group was vastly superior to the Halloran men. Only 4 percent at Halloran reached the critical score for trustworthiness (thirty-five pairs) while 69 percent at Getty did that well or better.

The study concluded that only 8 percent of those who took the test at Halloran were now "safe" Germans, while 78 percent at Getty were. But it also listed 7 percent at Getty as "unsafe" (75 percent at Halloran).

The "unsafe" men at Getty were found in all categories except the POW assistants. The largest number, predictably, were in the service company. Wetherill also showed a percentage of "unsafe" men. This was surprising considering the amount of screening involved in that program. The police school, it concluded, erred by 9 percent of their total selectees, and the administrative school by only 3 percent.

Howard Mumford Jones maintained that the success of the

administrative school at Getty derived from its aim, which was
not really to teach course material so much as it was to renew and
reteach the kind of faith each man must have in the honesty of
another. In that, the program undoubtedly made great gains.
But, he told the first graduating class in September 1945, if they
were still cynical about others, they could not be blamed. He
warned:

> Everything is against the success of this school. You are
> prisoners of war being taught by representatives of the
> enemy power, and you may very properly say you were
> defeated only by superior material force. . . . You may
> naturally conclude that the best way out of prison is to do
> what the jailor wants you to do, to seem to be what he wants
> you to be. You have had a large part of your work in a foreign
> language, a fact that has not made teaching and learning any
> easier. And you have perhaps seen no connection between
> American history and simple faith in human relationships,
> and no connection between military government and the
> ideals of a democratic state. Our studies here are imperfect,
> our teaching the best we can do under the circumstances,
> our classrooms and school equipment only what we could
> provide.

7 Fort Eustis

THE STATE DEPARTMENT MADE an agreement with France which required the War Department to turn over to that country all the German prisoners in the United States for use in construction after the war. Someone realized that the order meant that all the denazified men, trained in the glories of democracy, would spend months cooling their heels in France, becoming bitter, while Germany struggled to rebuild. The army decided to take a small step outside the State Department agreement.

Dr. Moulton explained: "What do you do if you're the army and you have a bunch of people you don't need now but you might need later? You set up a school to keep them around. That's what they did. That's really what Eustis was all about. We wanted to get some of these people directly back to Germany, where they might help in the military government and the occupation."

The Kearney, Getty, and Wetherill men were already on their way to direct repatriation, but they would hardly be enough. It was decided to find an additional twenty thousand trustworthy men and put them through a crash democratization course. From there, they would be directly repatriated to Germany. In December 1945, the program was pushed through the Pentagon in a matter of days by the hard work of a POWSPD team headed by Robert L. Kunzig. Kunzig recalls: "Here you had a situation where you wanted to set up a new program. They want it immediately—common sense dictates that anti-Nazis should go on a priority basis—and they also need all sorts of clearances in the military to begin something like this."

First, the SPD began an enormous screening program to select the men who would attend the special school. They couldn't send a man to each camp, so orders and directions were quickly sent to the AEOs and COs to pick their best. Screening began at once while work began, simultaneously, to get approval for the program.

Fort Eustis, Virginia, was designated as the site for the school. An entire antiaircraft battery had just moved out, leaving space available to house the men, run classes, and hold other activities. Even more in its favor was its proximity to East Coast ports, although, oddly, the graduates were sent to New York for embarkation rather than to the naval harbors at Hampton Roads, Newport News, or Norfolk.

But the mounds of paperwork had yet to clear. Kunzig recounted: "You have to clear it with all the interested parties— G1 was personnel, G2 would have an interest in intelligence, G4, supply, would have major input. Then you have to get all the subapprovals, then you have to get action from the top generals. It sits on desks, that's only human.

"This was late fall of 1945. It had been set up so the first load out of Eustis would go in February 1946. A group of us took it. We just went from one person to another, they call it 'walking through.'

"It was just a question of days. You could personally argue and persuade them and use whatever powers of persuasion one might have. Of course, the more you get, the better—it starts to snowball. So we moved it through, cars back and forth. We went to the Pentagon, then over to other places. We just lived this."

Once they pushed approval through the army brass, action began in earnest to get the school going on time.

Unfortunately, however, there was a small pro-Nazi POW camp at Eustis which colored the viewpoint of the base commander. He could not fathom how the special project could possibly run in a normal U.S. Army compound area. Kunzig recalls: "There was a colonel—a typical housekeeping officer. He was just horrified with all these damn Nazis. He said they didn't have the facilities—no barbed wire, guns, tanks. We tried to explain the situation as nicely as we could. It was an emergency! We wanted to start moving them in a few *days*. This was really action like they weren't used to."

Here, they had the ideal situation. Barracks after barracks was empty—there were mess halls, plenty of room for classes, and even for the large, planned lectures. The professors, ready to join the operation immediately, were coming down from the projects in Rhode Island. The men were being selected and shipped from all over the country. And they were face-to-face with a base commander who was totally uncooperative. He was refusing to allow them the use of his camp. Kunzig recalls: "I made a phone call to Washington, and he was removed the next day. The program could never have worked with this poor gentleman. He had no conception of what it was. To him, these were all nasty Nazis and should be lashed three times a day."

Alpheus Smith became the commanding officer, the role he had held at Getty. His entire team, with the exception of Howard Mumford Jones, who had left the program at Getty, arrived days later.

Obviously, considering the way they were selected, the process of finding the men to enter the Eustis project was very different from that used at the previous schools. On December 11, a letter had gone out to the commanding generals of each of the nine service commands making it their responsibility to see that the camps selected candidates for Eustis. Each had a quota ranging from six thousand for the Fourth Service Command to twelve hundred fifty for the First and Second. The prisoners themselves were to be chosen by the proper authorities within each camp. Only those who were cooperative and "favorably inclined toward democracy" would be chosen.

The selected prisoners had to qualify in at least one group of prewar anti-Nazis: those persecuted for religious, racial, or political reasons; those interned in concentration camps by the Nazis; former members of labor organizations opposed to the Nazis; former members of political parties in opposition to Hitler; or any prisoners who continued membership in an established church under Hitler. An additional test of their sincerity was their inclination to work for democratic purposes, as shown through their actions and attitudes in the camps.

Further qualifications deemed desirable were successful completion of a camp-level reeducation program, good health, and at least a minimal understanding of English. Naturally, all former members of the SS, SD, SA, Gestapo, Grepo (*Grenzpolizei*), Hitler Youth, as well as police directors, GFP (secret field police), and officers in assorted other hard-core Nazi organizations were automatically eliminated from consideration. Also rejected in advance were former members of the Nazi Party; members of the elite University Student Corps; anyone with the military rank of major or higher; all faculty and graduates of Napola, the Adolf Hitler Schools, or military academies; and members of the Neo-Pagan movement and of numerous other "spiritual" groups. Obviously, prisoners whose citizenship in Allied countries had been established were not eligible for Eustis, since they would not be repatriated to Germany or Austria.

Once selected, prisoners filled out a lengthy questionnaire prepared by the POWSPD with the Factory. These forms, the *Fragebogen*, were then evaluated by forty men at the Factory and compared with other screening material. Prisoners were divided into three groups—"white," "gray," and "black."

The "blacks" were unregenerate ex-Nazis. The screening

proved 13 percent of those tested fit that category. Three-fourths were labeled "gray." These were men who were generally non-political and who, it was felt, followed the leadership line like sheep. They were tested further before entering the school. The remaining men were classified as "white." They were definitely to be given the Eustis training. Figures from March 1946 showed that 83 percent of the men shipped to Eustis were ultimately approved as students.

With the war over and all German records in Allied hands, many men could be double-checked. At least one undesirable prisoner was uncovered this way. An intelligent officer who had completed a reeducation course in Texas, the man seemed perfect. However, an investigation in Berlin revealed that he was an early Nazi who had been sent to Spain by Hitler in 1936 to help organize Franco's air force.

When the prisoners reached Eustis, the whites were called to the Special Projects Center, the blacks went to the regular POW camp adjacent, and the grays were interviewed and reassessed. So many grays passed these further tests that two extra cycles were held to process them all, raising the total number of cycles to twelve. The original estimate of 20,000 men became in reality 25,338, of which 23,147 entered and completed the course.

With so many men being processed in so short a time, it was probably impossible to keep a few undesirables from sneaking through. Everything was moving so fast, Kunzig recalls, "I'm sure some of the twenty thousand must have been able to hide their allegiances." Once approved for the project, a man could still be rejected. In fact, 378 whites were reclassified black in the course of the program. But by and large the Eustis men were not inclined toward Hitler's paranoia.

Writer Quentin Reynolds spent several days at Eustis as a guest speaker. He made it a point to talk with and listen to the men. It was difficult at first because he remembered the unregenerate attitudes of many prisoners he had met in Europe a few months before and the concentration-camp scenes. "But gradually," he wrote, "I noticed something different about these Germans at Fort Eustis. Their eyes were clear—not sullen; they laughed at one another's jokes; there was nothing furtive about them. They . . . they . . . well, damn it all, they were different."

The students were required to bring with them several of the approved reeducation texts. On the list were the three booklets by Jones, any of the *Bucherreihe Neue Welt*, and two other POWSPD prepared volumes, *Kleiner Führer durch Amerika* and *Musik in Amerika*. A German-English dictionary and the Nevins-Commager pocket history—or another approved American history book—were also recommended.

The cycles took on the nickname "the six-day bicycle race." Each of twelve groups of roughly two thousand students would spend six days studying the workings of democracy and its potential for Germany. Then they would be off for home.

At the start of each cycle, the men were told that they would be returned directly to Germany. Despite the mere three-strand token fence around the compound, this incentive effectively eliminated the possibility of escape.

The reeducation purposes and content of the project were not hidden in any way. Alpheus Smith told the men in an orientation speech that there would be a good deal of talk about democracy in the lectures. The reason for this, he said, was that Americans believe in democracy and are convinced that everyone would be better off if the entire world were run democratically.

They were urged not to accept blindly what they were told. The emphasis was put on free and open discussion, questions, and ironing out objections. A basic tenet of democracy, they were told, is that "if John Smith has an idea which is sound, others will accept it in the long run *but* Smith must explain the idea to others in terms they can understand and they must make an honest effort to listen to what he says. If, after all this, they still don't accept his ideas, Smith should re-examine his plans because the fault is with him."

According to Commander Edwin Casady, the faculty estimated that the effectiveness of the Eustis program would depend on the effectiveness of the discussion groups. Authoritarianism had dominated every aspect of German life from the domineering father in the family circle to schoolteachers and political leaders. "If the re-orientation program had a definable objective," he wrote, "it was to overcome the reluctance to think for themselves that had been trained into these POWs."

Quentin Reynolds witnessed this happening all around the camps and commented: "At night I found groups of men sitting around. . . . I stood on the outskirts of their groups and listened. . . .

" 'Today Colonel Smith gave us quite a talk,' one was saying. . . . 'He admitted, much to our shocked surprise, that American democracy wasn't perfect. But he said the trouble was not with democracy but with some Americans. Some . . . American leaders and their followers, he said, ought to start practicing democracy. Then he told us about the great benefits Americans have.' "

Every day the students, divided into two groups of a thousand each, would attend two lectures, a film, and two discussion groups based on the lectures. In addition, time was set aside for private sessions on personal problems, mainly fears about repatriation. Another film was offered in the evening for those men who wished to attend, or they could use the time for recreational activities or other personal choices.

The personal-problems section dealt with hundreds of individual anxieties in each cycle. The questions raised by prisoners, which increased with each cycle, covered a wide range of subjects. Some were very personal: how to find their families; what had happened to their savings or property. Most of the men were anxious to know the physical condition of their hometown or region and what restrictions would be placed on life by the Allies.

Only two regular hours in each cycle could be scheduled for these sessions, but counselors were available at all times.

The contribution of this section was greater than anticipated, for it demonstrated to men who had historically been subservient to higher authority that they could ask questions of the authorities and receive answers and help. The problems section also published a daily current-events sheet, *Der Kurzbericht* ("The Brief Report"), summarizing world news of particular interest to the Germans.

The six-day schedule of the school was a marvel of logistics. Upon arrival at Eustis, the men were put into the "entrance pool." Only two thousand men could be processed in each cycle, but delays in transporting them in and out meant that four thousand to eight thousand men could actually be in the pool at any given time. A series of alternate programs had to be organized to occupy these men.

The only indispensable part of the pool program was the orientation lecture by Alpheus Smith which defined the school and its goals. As in the cycle itself, attendance at all scheduled activities before 5:00 P.M. was compulsory.

In the pool, the men daily (except Sunday) attended one hour of recorded music and one hour of filmstrips and specially selected films as mandatory class hours. The titles of the twelve lectures in the cycle were distributed to the men so that they could use their free time to do research in advance if they chose.

All the voluntary evening activities available to the men in the current cycle were open to pool members. In addition, a gym was set up and Ping-Pong tables were placed in the barracks.

The first lecture of the first day of the actual cycle, entitled "The Democratic Way of Life," was given by Dr. Moulton at 8:00 and 10:00 A.M. to groups of a thousand men. Its purpose was to explain that democracy is not just a political system but an attitude that guides all human relations. Stress was placed on the value of the individual and the equality of all human beings. Compromise and the ability to choose one's own course of action (by weighing alternatives) were emphasized as a key to living democratically. Naturally, this was considered the most important lecture, because it set the stage for the eleven to follow.

The first lecture was filled with "dreadfully simple" examples, according to Moulton. But it had to be simple because of the various educational and social backgrounds among the students.

It was given in German, like most lectures at Eustis. Moulton was the only American officer who was completely fluent in the language. "That was my particular value to the program," he said. While most of the lecture staff were German refugees or Kearney and Getty graduates, "there was a big advantage in having an officer like me on display as a native American who could actually speak German."

In the very first class he gave at Eustis, he recalled, "I came out and started the lecture, *'meine Herren.'* That means 'gentlemen.' And apparently this was one of the most effective things I did. I didn't even know what I was doing. But they hadn't been talked to that way for years. This was terribly effective."

Subjects covered in the first lecture were: "What is democracy?" "What are rights?" "What is the basic principle of democracy?" "How can free and equal men agree on any course of action?"

After the lecture—and after every lecture all week—the men, in groups of fifty, would attend a one-hour discussion session with a staff instructor. In these sessions many prisoners commented that before the lecture they had never understood that democracy was more than a political concept—that it involved behavior in all relationships. A nineteen-year-old student, Wilhelm T., said that the lecture reinforced ideas he had been mulling over for some time, since it showed him that democracy was an incarnation of his Christian beliefs. Many others agreed with him. "I was impressed with the exchange of opinion of all people, and not only adults," wrote one. "In the respect of the individual and mutual respect between worker and employer, there is only progress and development."

The first day's discussions were followed by the film *Abe Lincoln in Illinois*, chosen to show how in a free democratic society men develop to the best of their abilities. Despite problems with the lack of a German sound track, the film was well liked. The faculty, speculating on its popularity, thought it was because Lincoln's rise to power from near poverty was close to Hitler's own story.

Yet the response was broader than that. Prisoner Heinz R. praised Lincoln's human qualities and sincerity, calling him "a symbol that democracy is not weakness but strength." Others noted the chivalrous attitude of Lincoln's political adversaries and the important role of American women in family life and politics as depicted by Mrs. Lincoln (reinforced in later films by the two Mrs. Wilsons and Mrs. Roosevelt).

One of the discussion leaders also pointed out that while Lincoln was alive, Bismarck was preparing German unity through "blood and iron," and that the Revolution of 1848 might have pushed Germany to the way of democracy if it had succeeded.

After lunch and a personal-problems session, the men went on to the second lecture. Again the speaker was Dr. Moulton. This time his topic was "The Constitution."

The second lecture was the first example that the prisoners were given in any detail of the applicability of the ideals of democracy to an actual government. The discussion period afterward was doubled in length to accommodate the many questions. Students' comments reflected the recent German experience. They praised checks and balances as a way of preventing a dictatorship.

In the evening of the first day—and all six days—the programs were optional. They included lectures (mostly in German), discussion groups, round-table forums, or silent films from the Yale University Historical Society. The authoritarian Prussian state and Austria were among the lecture topics; discussions and forums, often with guests like Quentin Reynolds, were on such subjects as New York City, Austrian literature, and family problems.

One evening lecture, on rebuilding German youth, aroused very active debate on the question of whether youth movements should be politically oriented in the future. The discussion degenerated into heated arguments resulting from a generation gap which left the faculty with the feeling that Germans were a long way from tolerating free debate.

Other popular evening fare included a round-table discussion on the collective guilt of the German people and a lecture on labor law in the Germany of the future. The former, while considered an excellent topic for discussion by most of the prisoners, aroused immediate complaints from many that no agreement had been reached at the end of the debate. They would have preferred that a definite decision as to their guilt or innocence for the holocaust be determined. Germans do not like to be left with unfinished discussions. All, especially those who argued that there was collective guilt, were very frustrated but, since no absolute conclusion was at hand, most appeared to be especially delighted with the arguments against collective guilt.

The prisoners labeled the discussion after the labor lecture the "first serious political discussion" they had participated in in many years. Several commented later that it was this lecture which persuaded them to become involved with unionism after repatriation.

The film *Here Is Germany*, presented as an evening option during the later cycles, depicted the horrors of Nazi atrocities and the political attitudes which allowed Hitler to take power. It aroused heated discussions in which the majority always took the standard "we-didn't-do-it" approach. Many prisoners called it "an obstacle to international reconciliation," and they decried its failure to show the brutality meted out even to "Aryans" who didn't like the military or the harsh discipline of Nazism. On the other side, nearly as many demanded that it be shown all over Germany, calling it a "faithful portrait" and an "excellent lesson."

Church services were offered every night, as well as at least two entertainment films from the approved film circuit (admission charge: fifteen cents in POW coupons). The men also did a lot of reading on their own. Favorite library books were Wendell Willkie's *One World,* R. T. Clark's *The Fall of the German Republic,* and Arnold Brecht's *Prelude to Silence.* Novels by John Steinbeck and Thomas Mann were also in great demand.

The second day opened with Dr. Moulton's third lecture, "Political Parties, Elections, and Parliamentary Procedures." From the second and third lectures the prisoners learned, according to Wilfried S., "that there can be nothing superior to a government that is elected by the people, and which gives justice to all."

Dr. Moulton noted: "The important part of these two lectures was that we got across ideas in a way that wasn't phony. If we tried to play some kind of phony game, they would have been the first to catch onto it. It was all the more impressive to them because it wasn't phony."

After the subsequent discussion sessions, there were two films—*A Tuesday in November,* election day in a small American town, and *The River,* describing how floods on the Mississippi are combated.

There were few comments on these two films other than the observation that the one on elections showed the "humorous aspect" of American voting, which contrasted with the hostile tenseness of German politics as they remembered it. Concerning *The River,* several prisoners were impressed that even while planning for warfare the United States had also engaged in constructive projects that were not war-related.

The afternoon lecture, the fourth in the cycle, covered "Education in the United States"—the class they asked for but never got at Getty. Schools, Technical Sergeant Fourth Grade Strauss explained, are the training ground of a nation. He discussed the characteristics of schools in a democracy, local control of education, and the principle of free education for all through high school. The prisoners were highly impressed with the relaxed atmosphere of American schools, expressing openly the wish that they had attended schools in which they had not been subjected to authoritarian teachers. The majority spoke earnestly of how they would work to see that their children could enjoy classroom education and thus become self-reliant citizens rather than fearful subjects.

The third day began with another lecture by Dr. Moulton, this one on "The Economic Scene—I," the introduction to the sixth lecture, given in the afternoon by Technical Sergeant J. J. Neumaier, "The Economic Scene—II." Both lectures emphasized free enterprise and equal opportunity, and the reaction was tepid. The prisoners had few questions or comments.

The film for the third day was *American Romance*, the story of a Czech immigrant who, like Horatio Alger, rises from mere laborer to auto magnate through the opportunities available to him in the free U.S. democratic economy. Although it was criticized as unrealistic or "too capitalistic and materialistic" by the ardent anti-Fascists, the majority were awed by its impressive Technicolor photography, and found the idea of the poor immigrant making good appealing. Many prisoners commented that it was a pleasing example of "applied democracy." Fritz K. wrote: "It is a fairy tale but one which contains so many truths that it leaves a deep impression."

On the fourth day, the students turned to subjects they would most need in Germany. The morning lecture, "American Military Government," given by Staff Sergeant von Halle, was never one of the more popular offerings for obvious reasons. Nor were the documentary films that followed, and, in retrospect, they seem oddly unrelated to the main purpose of the school. The first was an OWI production on the Rural Electrification Administration entitled *Power and the Land*; the second, an *Army-Navy Screen Magazine* film, *Displaced Persons in Europe*. In cycles ten, eleven, and twelve, the latter was replaced with the more relevant *American Military Government in Cologne*, but none of the three particularly impressed the prisoners. Rural electrical power, especially, was regarded by most as "unlikely" in Germany, thus irrelevant for them.

"Democratic Traditions in Germany" was the afternoon lecture of the fourth day, in which Henry Ehrmann and Staff Sergeant Arnold Price attempted to convince the Germans that there was a tradition in their political history upon which democracy could be based. Reaction was favorable to this lecture, since the emphasis on the failures during the Weimar Republic rather than after 1933 gave the Germans another excuse not to be blamed. Indeed, many prisoners were pleased with what they called the "conciliatory tone" of the class.

Dr. Ehrmann spoke twice on the fifth day of each cycle with lectures on "Why the Weimar Republic Failed." It was a detailed study of a negative topic. As Ehrmann wrote in his lecture notes: "Only if we know the real reasons for the failure can we learn the lessons necessary for future guidance and preserve many of the positive accomplishments of the republican era."

The lectures were long and very detailed, tracing the compromises made to begin the Weimar Republic and the reasons for their failures—the attitudes of the army, the radical right, the judiciary, and government leaders. The political roles of industry and the large landowners were also followed in their contribution to the fall of the Weimar Republic. Since the compromises failed on all sides, Ehrmann said, the republic couldn't possibly survive. The students uniformly appreciated having the "gaps in their knowledge of facts" filled. They also saw this as the lecture that was most relevant to Germany's future. Several suggested that it should have been the opening lecture, since it afforded them a more objective comparison between the American and Weimar constitutions.

A surprisingly large number of men said that the Weimar lecture was the justification for conducting a thorough reeducation program to cure the "German sickness." "I had the impression from the lecture that the Americans topped us by far in inner value," wrote one graduate. Naturally, a few felt exactly the opposite, that these facts proved that the people are helpless against evil forces.

To coordinate with the new depression the prisoners were expected to feel after the Weimar lectures, the personal-problems section extended discussions of current Germany and held an "individual-interviews" hour that day.

The Seventh Cross was then shown, a film based on Anna Segher's novel describing an anti-Nazi's escape from a concentration camp. It was hoped that the film would encourage a positive outlook among the men by complementing the lectures which stressed a rediscovery of good traditions in Germany itself. The theme pointed out the kernel of good in all human beings and the ability of the little man to do something if he tries. Yet, perhaps as praise, most prisoners saw this as an example of "American cultural life" rather than a universal idea.

"The World of Today and Germany," a lecture by Technical Sergeant Fourth Grade Strauss, opened the morning for the prisoners on their last day. This is one world, he told them, and the great nations must renounce both isolationism and imperialism so the world as a whole can be operated democratically. "I have learned," remarked one prisoner of this lecture, "that the little man in America is not so very different from the little man in Germany. He too complains about his government, about being in the Army, about his officers. Since all the little people are so similar, why can't we live in peace?"

Commander Casady recalled another POW reaction which occurred in a discussion group after the lecture. The POW obviously suddenly reached a conclusion that amazed him and, "his face revealing his astonishment at his discovery, burst forth with: 'What the world needs is for more people to try to understand more people more.' "

The last two required documentaries were both from the OWI—*TVA*, the story of the Tennessee Valley Authority, and

Toscanini. In the latter, one of the most popular films of the cycle because of the music ("Foreign music is good"), the conductor is shown as a refugee from Fascism leading the NBC Philharmonic in Verdi's "Hymn of Nations."

In the final class, "New Democratic Trends," given by Dr. Ehrmann, he posed the question: "Can democracy solve the complex social and economic problems of the modern world?" The prisoners could be left only with the positive feeling that yes, democracy probably was the best answer.

The last hour was devoted to graduation exercises. In a formal ceremony, Alpheus Smith represented the army, and two prisoners spoke for the men. A guest speaker from the Provost Marshal General's Office or a university congratulated the students, and certificates were awarded to all the graduates. As a finale, Stephen Vincent Benét's "Prayer for the United Nations" was read at each ceremony.

The activities in the "exit pool" were very flexible. Scheduled programs were canceled 90 percent of the time in order to meet last-minute train schedules. The only required activity was the screening of the film *Wilson*, the biography of the twenty-eighth president. Several prisoners commented that the Wilson and Lincoln films gave them a truthful picture of the American people: "freedom and peace-loving, but strong when they feel their ideals threatened." A sample week in the exit area showed a schedule of entirely feature films, documentaries, and music.

The success of Eustis was not just in the course content. The POWSPD felt that the Germans, with their exaggerated respect for order, neatness, and organization, needed to be shown that we could obtain order without giving up individual freedom. They learned this lesson through the class work, the well-planned schedule, and the relationship they had with the faculty.

Action to make everything run smoothly never ceased. The staff worked tirelessly. Almost every night after the evening activities were done, Henry Smith, T. V. Smith, Moulton,

Casady, and Ehrmann gathered at Alpheus Smith's home to make any necessary adjustments.

They discussed individual student problems, problems in administration, new methods of teaching, and changes in courses. Quentin Reynolds sat in on one of these sessions when he taught there. He recalled:

"I've got an idea," Colonel Smith would say quietly. "Let's toss it around. Tear it to pieces boys."

And the boys would, and soon something new and constructive would come out of it. As they argued heatedly, rank was forgotten. This was a group of highly intelligent men, each completely nuts about the work he was doing, each with perhaps highly individual ideas, but each knowing that the success of the program depended upon the cumulative talents of them all rather than the individual ideas of any of them. They finished at 2 A.M. exhausted, but they accomplished something.

Most probably the group would discuss teaching methods, which were regularly adapted to needs. "The main effort should not be wasted in teaching *against* something," said Alpheus Smith. Rather, they should be teaching *for* something—the broadening of the prisoners' education.

The faculty also studied responses to a student questionnaire. Of those answering the question about the success of the course, 98 percent in the first two cycles and 99 percent in the third to fifth cycles responded affirmatively.

In direct questions about the lectures themselves, "Why the Weimar Republic Failed" consistently got the highest number of votes as the best class (49 percent). Next highest was "The Democratic Way of Life," with 16 percent. Fifteen percent liked "The World of Today and Germany." But these questions were answered before the last lecture, and, from spot checks that were made, it would probably have won the vote hands down.

Of the films, *American Romance* was the first choice, clearly showing the effectiveness of disguised propaganda in films. *Abe Lincoln in Illinois* and *Toscanini* also scored well. And while 30 percent liked *The Seventh Cross*, a strong minority objected to it for various reasons.

Eighty-five percent expressed satisfaction with the help given them by the personal-problems section. The one man who couldn't cope and committed suicide would always remain a distressing failure to the staff. The most common complaint was that the section was poorly informed about Austria and the zones of occupation other than the American zone.

Many prisoners requested copies of the lectures and other written material, expressing a belief that such material would enable them to "spread the gospel" among their compatriots at home.

When asked to compare Eustis to their previous camp, the majority lauded the freedom (*"Mehr Freiheit"*), but the first cycle complained about the poor canteen (which was not fully open until the second cycle). Other complaints ranged from lack of heat to poor food, but, in general, the prisoners felt the mental stimulation compensated admirably for the physical discomforts, and a number of prisoners even wrote "Many thanks for the opportunity" on their questionnaires.

Supply problems *had* created shortages, and in the first few cycles menus were felt to be inadequate by students and faculty alike. Casady used his naval connection frequently to get the American staff into nearby Camp Peary for a good meal and even composed a song immortalizing the situation. It began:

> *I've got those empty belly blues.*
> *I've got those empty belly blues.*
> *For I'm from Fort Eustis,*
> *Got mud on my shoes.*
> *When evenings I'm weary,*
> *I go to Camp Peary*

To get a square meal.
Christ, what a deal!

That the Eustis program was successful was made evident to
the staff in many ways. The eager participation in the discussion
periods and their continuation in the barracks after class, the
heavy use of libraries, the attentiveness during classes, and the
outspoken assurance that what they were learning would be put
to use in Germany showed that many were truly using the opportunity to learn what the army hoped they would learn. Or, at the
very least, they seemed to be eager to learn and improve
themselves.

In an unsolicited letter, a prisoner in the sixth cycle wrote:

If I had been the speaker at the final exercises I would not
have preached hate against the Third Reich, would not have
hinted at concentration camps . . . although I fully agree
justice must be done.

I would have spoken about the "new," . . . the fact that
Germany, Europe, and the whole world are to be conquered
in this spirit, that a new life has to be led. . . . Our task lies
not in remembering the Third Reich. Our task lies in acting
for the future. . . . A new spirit must be created—a spirit
that has a powerful support in the potential tremendous
production of modern times.

What was this new spirit being stressed in the classes?
Nearly every German commencement speaker echoed the words
of the speaker in the fourth cycle who professed: "Our vow to
rebuild an anti-Fascist, a better, a peaceful Germany and Austria
may be at the same time our gratitude toward those progressive
people in the U.S.A. who helped us perceive this aim.

"Together with them, as cosmopolitans of the atomic era, we
will work unflaggingly to build up a world in which the principles
of the United Nations will become a reality."

Several polls, student course evaluations, and social studies were taken of the men who passed through Eustis. Many of them still exhibited a fear of revealing their true feelings, something they'd learned under Nazi oppression. Nevertheless, the studies did indicate some things about their attitudes.

Tests showed that age made very little difference in attitude. However, the younger men, having matured in Hitler's Germany, were more confused. Catholics appeared to be more humanitarian than Protestants. A larger percentage of Catholics deplored the mistreatment of Jews and other minorities merely because they were human beings, without attempting to find economic or political justifications for treating all people well.

Older men frequently took the position that all the young were hopelessly trained in Nazism and needed great reorientation. The young, on the other hand, blamed Hitler's rise to power on their elders, who, they felt, were immoral as a group. This generation gap was apparent in the many clashes and debates that took place during discussion classes.

While all of the prisoners expressed strong pro-democratic and pro-American sentiments, most appeared unwilling in psychological tests to grasp the real meaning of participating in the running of a country. The desire to be nonpolitical, to be exonerated from any responsibility for policy, actions, or events still ran strong. Perhaps this is no different from the American attitude manifested by less than 50 percent of the eligible voters participating in certain elections, but it did not leave the analysts overly optimistic about the future of a democratic Germany.

A far more positive view appeared in the course evaluations by the POWs of their classes. In those responses, the younger men, now rid of Nazism, showed a high degree of eagerness to learn and grow intellectually. The significance the prisoners gave to the "eternal-vigilance" aspects of democracy refutes the psychological study's pessimism, and a vast majority said the most important lesson of the cycle was never to follow the "Pied Piper" again.

Student comments supported the viewpoint of the sociologists that the most convincing argument to the new converts was that democracy could be a successful and practical way of life. "Democracy means good living," they wrote. Their frank, utilitarian approach exemplified the German tendency to measure every *Weltanschauung* ("conception of the world from a specific standpoint") in terms of the success it can demonstrate, especially on an economic level. American democracy was economically, politically, and socially successful; therefore, they would give it a try.

Opinion was divided among the prisoners themselves as to whether there actually had been an awakening of political acuity and vigilance in the majority of their fellow-students. Some complained that discussions in the barracks showed most men to be reckless conformists and opportunists who, even when adopting democratic terminology, had lost nothing of their rigidity, arrogance, and tenseness. John Hasslacher commented in retrospect that in most class discussions the American instructors "had a bad time arguing with the Communists and anti-militarists." These same anti-Fascists and Communists, he added, ran the camp during his cycle and appeared to be the "only ones to 'profit' from the free, laissez-faire exchange of ideas." "I didn't learn anything I had not known before," he remembered.

Werner B. agreed, writing that the only thing he learned in American camps, including Fort Eustis, was "how to pick oranges." But others pointed to a significant change in the general attitude of many of the men. Barracks give-and-take tended to center around politics rather than the usual endless rehash of daily worries. And the overcoming of mutual distrust was very evident, thanks to the general atmosphere of goodwill that prevailed during the cycles.

It was, of course, impossible for polls and tests to predict how lasting any attitude change might be. As Alpheus Smith pointed out, "We send back to Germany only those who we believe are really democrats in their hearts. We hope that in their home towns they run for office; we hope that those who are teachers and artists will exert their influence on their pupils. We could be wrong. We're not claiming anything. Let's say we're hopeful without being too optimistic."

When the men had completed the Eustis cycle, they were immediately sent home. Most were moved by train to New York, where they boarded Victory ships, with POWSPD instructors and former AEOs as escort officers. The latter began their real work in France, seeing to it that their special prisoners were kept separate from the regular POWs and cleared through to Germany as expeditiously as possible. The situation in France was rugged, at best, for all war prisoners. One advance escort officer wrote to Alpheus Smith: "The PWs at Fort Eustis should be warned to expect rather rough treatment when they reach the ETO, despite their special status. Accommodations for all prisoners at Camp Bolbec are very primitive."

Things were not much better in the havoc that was unreconstructed 1946 Germany. "We would get them there, turn them loose, and they would face misery. But at least they'd be in Germany," sighed Dr. Moulton.

Since the army opted for wide press coverage of the Eustis project, the March 6, 1946, graduation exercises were attended by a group of correspondents brought down from Washington on a press sortie. General Bryan, by then provost marshal general, called the school an "effort to make of selected Germans a sort of spear for democratic ideas in Germany."

Follow-up newspaper coverage of Eustis, Kearney, Getty, and Wetherill graduates was also encouraged by the War Department. After he returned to the United States, Kunzig wrote a piece for *American* magazine describing the democratic activities of his former prisoners in Stuttgart. *The New York Times* and other newspapers carried many short articles about how captives schooled in the United States were helping to run Germany. All the news was very favorable to the program.

The Factory at Fort Kearney had closed as the Eustis school

was beginning. A few of the remaining men had, months earlier, become instructors at the Getty and Wetherill projects. Ten were sent as teachers to the administrative school at Querqueville, France, which was hastily established by Davison and Schoenstedt in the summer of 1945 for reorientation purposes. Most of the Kearney men had been repatriated in the fall of 1945, but thirty-six were sent to Eustis and repatriated with the early cycles from there.

By February 15, 1946, only the men needed to put out the last two editions of *Der Ruf* remained at Kearney, and the paper, which had also been distributed in camps in France after V-E Day, ceased publication with its twenty-sixth issue (dated April 1, 1946, four days before the last cycle graduated at Eustis, but actually published one month earlier).

The last group left Fort Eustis on April 8, 1946. The departure signaled the end of prisoner-related work for most of the faculty. Moulton, Henry Smith, and others went to see the last group off on the train. As they stood watching, a prisoner spotted Smith, waved, and called, "Let's face it, Major. There's no future in the PW business!"

# Evaluating the Program

WHEN ASKED WHETHER the reeducation program had been a success, one of the SPD directors wrote, in jest:

> Many people will ask, of course, whether the prisoners have actually changed. The easiest answer to this is photographs taken before and after their captivity. Obviously, they have gained considerable weight. But it is our firm conviction that they have also become aware of the spiritual powers of this great country. Go into any camp and you will find them jitterbugging to the latest recording of America's great jazz, or perhaps with an ear cocked attentively to the radio from which the humanitarian and courageous career of Ma Perkins is being expounded. And certainly most of them know that there is only one superman and that he is an American reporter on the *Daily Planet*.

One could argue that there is a lot of truth in that sarcastic statement—a touch of the best and worst of the program. Although the program was not wildly acclaimed, the degree of response among the Germans to the AEOs' efforts surprised even the experts.

In his book *Is Germany Incurable?* psychiatrist Dr. Richard M. Brickner labeled Germany a culture of paranoid people, and he seriously doubted that any outside source could achieve much in the way of reeducation with people who were the product of such an insecure tradition. The outside world should stay away, he said. The only thing it could do, perhaps, was locate the few nonparanoid members of the society and encourage them to act as catalysts for mass therapy as a postwar cure for Nazism. There was no way, he argued, to "render harmless individual sources of paranoid contagion within Germany." The world could only help those who were marginally sick to join the few healthy Germans by teaching them new values. Beyond that, he wrote, not even a "clinical psychiatrist should try to go."

Without using psychiatric terms like *paranoia*, this is precisely what the reeducation program had attempted to do: to help the non-Nazis and marginal Nazis adopt democratic values through the introduction of new ideas (new for the Germans) and broader concepts. But as Brickner pointed out and Henry Ehrmann reaffirmed in an article in a sociological journal, great care was necessary.

Had the values of democracy been associated with the defeat and failure of the German Army, their pride could have turned them toward a new Hitler to give them back the self-esteem they lost in defeat (as after World War I, when Germans believed they had been sold out, not militarily beaten). Democracy could not be forced down their throats, from victor to vanquished. It had to be presented in such a manner that the prisoners could accept it as a hope for Germany and not an Allied directive.

A subtle, soft-sell approach was the safest method. The SPD had attempted to keep it a voluntary renaissance of ideas, an opening of new avenues. It had generally avoided pressure tactics and overt persuasion. (Of course, there is no way of knowing exactly what each AEO did, but their orders were to avoid pressuring, and thus possibly antagonizing, prisoners.)

Virtually every sociologist or psychologist who studied the reeducation program and the possibility of reeducating Germany was skeptical, agreeing that there was great danger involved in such a program. The primary danger was that of leaning too much on the American, British, or French experience rather than on German sources. There was also the danger of force-feeding instead of winning them to democracy by teaching them to discriminate between fact and propaganda.

Even though the planners worked very hard to avoid the worst pitfalls by relying on the democratic traditions in German history and free access to all media as central segments of the program, America was often the focus. Thus, observers from outside the army who frequently wrote of the faults in the program claimed it was not scientific enough and too much was drawn from the American experience. It was being handled by poets, lawyers, and language experts rather than by sociologists or psychologists (the sociologists and psychologists said). The only firsthand knowledge of Germany came from the German refugees, who themselves came from the deficient, if not paranoid, Aryan culture.

Most "experts" viewed the reeducation program as an experiment that, although not what they would have preferred, just might act as a proving ground. Using the prisoners as guinea pigs, behavioral and social scientists could discover what would really be needed to reeducate millions in postwar Germany. As educator and sociologist Curt Bondy wrote in 1944: "If the educational work in the camps should prove positive, these experiences should have an enormous influence on the whole reconstruction work, and should make a real contribution towards establishing a lasting peace."

As an answer to skeptics, and for their own edification, the POWSPD authorized a poll to measure various levels of reorientation. In the poll, Eustis graduates were compared to prisoners from Camp Atlanta, Nebraska, and Camp Shanks, New York.

Atlanta was a normal POW camp with a regular reeducation program and a mixed group of "whites," "grays," and "blacks." The men at Shanks represented an average group of POWs from all over the country who passed through the camp on the way to ships in New York. Many of the 22,153 men tested at Shanks resented the fact that they had not been chosen for Getty or Eustis, so their responses may have been colored. However, the tests did indicate the levels of reeducation fairly well and showed notable differences between the groups.

The Eustis group was found to be significantly more favorably disposed to democratic ideals than other prisoners. Either the crash course at Eustis was a necessary addition to the regular program in order to fully realize the goal, or the men selected for the project really were the best possible choices. Henry Ehrmann argued that the former was the case—that more than the camp programs was needed to truly proselytize democracy. Others felt that perhaps the difference was partly a result of both factors. In any event, considering where most prisoners stood when they arrived in the United States, the strong pro-democratic figures at Atlanta and even at Shanks showed a remarkable achievement by the POWSPD.

Ninety-six percent at Eustis said they preferred a democracy as the future German government, compared with 62 percent of the Shanks group. At Eustis, too, age seemed to make little difference, while at Shanks the highest number of unfavorable responses came from the group that had received the most Nazi education—those under thirty. (Only about 55 percent of this group wanted democratic rule.) Prisoners over thirty seemed more denazified as a group, perhaps because they could better remember Germany before Hitler.

In responses to other questions, the range was similar. Did they still believe Germans to be the master race? At Eustis 98 percent replied in the negative, compared with 90 percent at

Atlanta and 79 percent at Shanks. Would they fight the same war again? No, said 98 percent at Eustis, 89 percent at Atlanta, and 76 percent at Shanks. At Shanks 16 percent still believed that Germans were unsuited for democracy, compared with 1 percent at Eustis and 9 percent at Atlanta.

From the examiners' viewpoint, the least favorable responses, and the most distressing, in the poll came to the question: "Do you believe that Jews were the cause of Germany's troubles?" Even at Eustis a disquieting number (10 percent) said they felt Jews were at least partly to blame. At Shanks 49 percent agreed. An even higher percentage of those under thirty (55 percent) put a portion of the blame onto the Jews. Concluding that this attitude paralleled the American experience, one examiner wrote: "This is the most difficult of the undemocratic attitudes to dispel."

From the poll, analysts came to several conclusions about the success of the reeducation program. Approximately 75 percent of the German prisoners, they determined, left the United States with an appreciation of the value of democracy and a friendly attitude toward their captors. Only 15 percent were still not favorably disposed toward either America or democracy, and the rest were undecided. Considering the sullen, suspicious, and contemptuous attitudes of the prisoners upon arrival, in most cases, this was a noteworthy achievement in itself.

It was estimated that one-third of the departing prisoners were definitely anti-Nazi (double the number who arrived with that attitude) and pro-democratic, while 10 percent were still militantly Nazi (a slightly smaller percentage than among the arrivals).

If the estimates are at all reliable, it would appear that the general reeducation program was surprisingly effective. Possibly one-fourth of the men were reeducated to strong anti-Nazi beliefs and 60 percent moved to a positive attitude toward democracy as a direct result of what they learned in the camps. Unfortunately, only about 3 percent, at best, of the ardent Nazis were converted. But in Dr. Brickner's terms, that is a surprisingly large number.

Many sociologists who studied groups of prisoners were more cautious than the poll analysts, arguing that there was really no way to record precisely how many had been converted to democracy. They pointed out that Germans did not see Nazism as the vicious policy that it was until we forced them to recognize it as such. The most accepted parts of National Socialism among the masses had been its democratic aspects: no unemployment, a higher standard of living, national economic revival, higher wages, economic security, social welfare, health services, housing, parks, elimination of class distinctions, and so on. The people conveniently ignored its blacker side. Questioning of prisoners during the war showed that Hitler's credibility varied directly with his actions in those areas. Germans were willing to put up with living under Gestapo rule to have a quality of life previously out of their reach.

Sociologists also reminded the SPD of the pamphlet *What About the German Prisoner?* which it had issued in November 1944. The pamphlet was meant to give POW camp personnel a political picture of Germans and described the levels of Nazi adherence and what a true anti-Nazi or non-Nazi was. The sociologists referred the SPD back to its own discussion of "March Violets," the Nazi term for opportunists who jump on the winning side.*

The SPD had written: "All signs indicate that there are many 'March Violets' among the prisoners of war. It would be a mistake to classify them as non-Nazis just because they are not fanatics. However, the opportunists are different, they know when the game is up and become opportunists again. . . . At the right mo-

---

März Veilchen ("March Violet") or *März Gefallenen* ("March Fallen") were Nazi terms for those who had climbed on the bandwagon after Hitler came to power in 1933.

ment, they will take proper steps to announce a shift in allegiance."

There was no way the SPD could determine how many of the prisoners were "March Violets" who merely changed their allegiance once they saw Hitler losing and the Allies winning. The SPD could not even honestly claim that any prisoners had really been converted. Maybe all of them opportunistically realized that they could get both the socioeconomic rewards they had gained under the Nazis and the freedom of life they saw that the Americans had if they played along with the Allies. There was no sure way to tell. One could only wait to see what happened when the POWs got back to Germany. But the opinion polls and personal observations did prove that the prisoners believed that the United States provided prosperity and personal freedom for *all* and that they liked what they saw.

The detractors were right about one thing: if there was any failure in the overall program, it was that the prisoners learned to like America too much. Hundreds filed for immigration visas for themselves and their families as soon as they reached Germany. Many had been offered jobs by the Americans who employed them as prisoners, and so were able to return. Whether or not they had job offers, those who did immigrate apparently had such fond memories of their prison life that they settled within a few miles of the camps they'd been in.

In 1955 a group of successful German businessmen chartered a plane in Frankfurt for a nostalgic trip to Camp Trinidad, Colorado, their home away from home a decade earlier. There they were warmly welcomed, they laid wreaths on the graves of prisoners who had been reburied in the regular camp cemetery when the POW areas were eliminated, and then they flew home. As Rudolf Werner, a Trinidadite and a member of the West German Parliament from 1959 to 1972, remembered: "I cannot but admit that in Camp Trinidad there was quite a particular and pleasant atmosphere—if one forgets the main fact of being a prisoner. And since most people were young they made the best of that time. . . . It was rather 'magic mountain.' "

Even though the Eustis-Shanks-Atlanta poll showed 75 percent of the prisoners to have democratic tendencies after reeducation, the SPD was eager to study the strengths and weaknesses of the many sections of the program. As one measure, a survey of AEOs and observers was made as soon as the program officially ended to discover the positive and negative elements and the effects, if any, of unavoidable army bureaucracy on the program.

On the plus side, the AEOs felt the *Neue Welt* books and *Der Ruf* were very successful. Although the majority felt *Der Ruf* was perhaps *too* intellectual for the average prisoner, most agreed the reading material was generally well received. The number of reorders of the *Neue Welt* books particularly attested to the enthusiastic level of their reception in the camps.

The AEOs also commented that the English-language classes were very successful, particularly the spoken-English method of teaching. While history, geography, and civics classes were not so well rated, AEOs noted that when those courses were taught as discussion sections they were "the most effective educational medium in the repertoire." Guest lecturers also scored high marks.

The AEOs disagreed on how and why the religion program worked, although all believed it had great value in reeducation. Some of them felt religion should be separate from the AEO's responsibilities and simply have his benevolent support. Others felt they could work successfully with the chaplains. Perhaps the different attitudes were due to personalities, since the SPD had encouraged the latter method, arguing, "Religion is a very powerful influence with the majority of the human race. Its principles are consistent with those of democracy." It is our ally, they concluded.

The film program got mixed reviews as a medium. Many AEOs complained that the Signal Corps, which insisted on running the national film circuit for the SPD, inundated them with war films, boring the prisoners and causing a drop in attendance. AEOs who did not have that problem reported up to 92 percent attendance at film showings.

The effectiveness of the film program did decrease once the Signal Corps got into the act. Films selected by the AEOs on their own, either from the Factory list or from their own assessment of proper content, received an overwhelmingly better response from the prisoners and were more carefully planned to complement the reeducation program.

When the War Department horned in on the film program, it caused other problems for the SPD, too. The upper-level decision that the film program be coordinated from Washington rather than by the SPD and the AEOs in the field added 50 percent more paperwork to an already heavy load. An SPD self-evaluation reported: "Either 5 cents too much was submitted or the AEO forgot to personally sign the authenticating report. Now surely there's no excuse for such carelessness . . . but it should have been no great problem for responsible authorities in Washington to arrange to dispose of the 5 cents or to correct other irregularities, thereby conserving a mountain of paper and avoiding the harvest of disdain . . . and cynical amusement which permeates both service command and camps."

Given the decision on their own, the SPD would have let the AEOs select the films from an approved list and merely set up guidelines for selecting others, thereby keeping the paperwork to a minimum and in the camps themselves.

A more serious problem the SPD faced, thanks to the army, was the rather unfortunate coinciding of the new restrictions on food after V-E Day with the main reeducation drive. Prisoners could no longer buy beer or cigarettes unless they worked, and less food was served at mealtime. Although the army claimed that the restrictions on food came in response to a greater need among the troops abroad, the POWs regarded the changes as acts of "cowardly reprisal" contrary to the spirit, if not the letter, of the Geneva Convention, and certainly inconsistent with the democratic traditions we were trying to impress upon them.

To make matters worse, the press almost simultaneously began reporting the alleged Santa Claus-like treatment of German prisoners in Russia. These reports, which were later found to be the erroneous rantings of the Soviet propaganda machine, caused a sudden growth of pro-Communist activity among the POWs that helped complicate the AEOs' work considerably. As an SPD commentary noted: "The coincidence helped only the special projects commissar of the USSR."

Another major AEO criticism of the program was its segregation policy. It had "no teeth in it," they said, and never fully satisfied the demands of the reeducation effort. AEOs persisted in having problems with Nazis they could not transfer out of the camps because they could not get transportation and relocation cooperation from the War Department.

But none of these problems appears to have threatened the program as much as the War Department's own peculiarly destructive attitude toward the project. It is amazing that the SPD managed to achieve the remarkable results it did, considering the obstacles the War Department laid in its path. In early 1945, the secretary of war became aware that because of the variables within each service command and in the quality of AEOs, the program differed in magnitude from camp to camp. It also clearly went beyond the original, patronizing intent of the War Department. Regardless of the success to date of the project, the secretary wanted uniformity. General Lerch, the provost marshal general, was urged to step in to direct it in a more "military" fashion.

Orders went out to move SPD headquarters from New York to Washington, where it could be more closely supervised by the War Department. Lerch began putting names of key SPD personnel on lists of those available for transfer to the Pacific or

Europe. A civilian clerical staff was brought in which had to be trained from scratch in mid-program. The capable SPD staff was pared to the bone.

Of major concern to the SPD was Lerch's effort to control *Der Ruf*. With 372,000 prisoners to reeducate, he refused to understand the need to publish more than thirty-five thousand copies. This meant that Nazi leaders in many camps were able to dispose of the newspaper because only a few copies were received. If each camp had received several hundred copies, the Nazis could not have prevented its circulation, and its effectiveness would have been much greater and much accelerated. Finally, in July 1945, after a day of pleading by Acting Director McKnight (while Davison was at the school in Querqueville, France), Lerch agreed to print fifty thousand copies of each edition. (Eventually, the number reached seventy-five thousand.)

While Davison was still in France, Lerch tried to force a change in the content of *Der Ruf*. He wanted "less Thomas Mann and Stefan Zweig and more Henry Ford and General Knudsen." This would have been a disaster, making the paper nothing more than a blatant propaganda sheet. The SPD, led by McKnight, managed to hold him off.

Of all the hurdles put in the SPD's path by the War Department, none was more potentially damaging to its work than the inexplicable "Red scare" that was begun in early 1945 by a colonel (who shall remain nameless here) in the Counter Intelligence Division (CID).

CID security checks were common in the army during the war. From 1937 to 1946, more than three million people—civilian and military—were checked for Nazi or Communist leanings. In 1944, the army gave all its investigators the alleged plans for the Communist "world revolutionary movement," as envisioned by the New York City police. Among the hundreds of groups listed as Communist-infiltrated to some degree, thus making their members suspect, were the YMCA, YMHA, United Auto Workers, American Newspaper Guild, Jewish schools, and the student councils of over two hundred colleges.

In May 1945, the army had nearly 1,400 agents on duty screening suspected Fascists and Communists. All it took to get on the list was one complaint against you from a superior officer or, in the case of civilians, a civilian source. Of 952 individuals investigated in July 1945, only 216 were readily cleared.

Naturally, the SPD could not escape scrutiny. The check for possible Reds was an ongoing process during its entire existence. General Lerch was assured by the McCarthyite colonel in the CID that there was grave danger to the program and his own survival in the military if all of the personnel were not absolutely lily-white (meaning, of course, no shades of pink or red!). The situation built to the inevitable explosion.

On April 14, a loyalty check was ordered on all thirty-one members of the SPD's headquarters staff. Next to several names on the list there were notations suggesting that they were particularly questionable. The men who were marked "suspect" included two men who have since become respected educators, and two loyal, active, conservative Republicans (also with distinguished careers since the war).

Eventually, three men were pulled out of the SPD—without notice—for alleged, but never documented or proved, left-wing leanings. The transfer of one of these, the executive officer holding things together in the wake of Lerch's reorganization attempts, led to a big shake-up within the office.

Both Colonel Davison and Captain Schoenstedt were in France working with the Querqueville project. Maxwell McKnight, acting director in Davison's absence, had gone to Fort Getty on inspection. The CID men made their move.

McKnight wrote to Davison:

Yesterday, in my absence, without the slightest prior indication, —— received orders for overseas duty. . . . Under the

present trying circumstances, this series of incidents indicative of mistrust and lack of understanding became intoler-
able. I telephoned in my request for relief from my duties as
Acting Director, which was readily accepted. . . .

Howard [Mumford Jones] has also reached the breaking
point. His letter to Gen. Lerch really means business this
time. . . .

The I & E Division* and all its personnel is much
distrusted. If —— weathers the present red scare cleanup,
I'll be surprised.

. . . Because of the prisoners it is important for —— to
stay on the job but will they understand that in Washington?
I played the only card I had in the hopes that sufficient
understanding might be achieved to last until you returned.
If I couldn't protect ——, *Der Ruf*, etc, as Acting Director
there seems to be little sense in my remaining in that
capacity.

Two days later, McKnight wrote with more bad news:

. . . General Lerch explained the difficulties that he faced
concerning the grave risk to the program and himself if
personnel were not snow-white. . . . He asked me to stay on
as Deputy Director and to go to Getty Monday to try to
persuade Howard to stay on too. . . . I will have to carry
tidings that —— and ——, both of whom Colonel Alpheus
[Smith] desperately needs and wants and who were shaken
loose from I & E after great effort by Col. Alpheus, failed to
clear the [name of CID colonel] test and therefore will not be
assigned to the PMG. . . . —— is on the rampage again and

---

*Information and Education Division, General Frederick Osborn's section, which
ran American officer training and language schools and which had given birth, indirectly,
to the reeducation program. Much of the faculty came from Osborn's schools.

the adamant view of the highest people on top-side at the War Department is the job will go by the board. . . .

Undoubtedly, —— must have gotten an intelligence report—probably that he subscribed to the New Republic.

Howard Mumford Jones, fed up with losing precious time and faculty because of CID clearance problems, resigned from the program at Getty in the middle of the first class. He gave several trivial reasons, including War Department refusal to remove the barbed wire from around the residential barracks of the prisoners and a desire to return to Harvard, but the proverbial straw was the rejection of two eminently well qualified faculty members because the CID thought they were too "liberal."

The remaining faculty united behind McKnight to fight the removal of key men from headquarters and to try to get the temporarily appointed acting director (Davison stayed in Europe for a while longer, and McKnight was reinstated as deputy director only) to work with them on friendly terms. In a telephone call to one of General Lerch's aides, McKnight argued: "The absence of Colonel Davison and Captain Schoenstedt, the moving of the division to Washington, the breaking in of an entirely new group of civilian personnel, paring the division to the bone to provide personnel for screening, the taking on of much additional work in connection with the Getty and Wetherill projects, indicate some of the many difficulties too numerous to mention. ——, as acting executive officer, has been the one officer above all others who made it possible to carry on in the present situation. After such an example of devotion to duty and loyalty, the manner in which this officer was removed from the division will have serious repercussions on the morale of all division personnel.

"In addition, he is the only officer in the programs branch available for duty in Washington. Without him it is difficult to figure how *Der Ruf* can continue to be regularly published in its present form."

It was a vain effort to protect the men so badly needed.

The situation in regard to the approval of faculty for Getty, Wetherill, and Eustis was a disaster. Every instructor, but especially the historians, who were most suspect, had to be cleared by the CID. The fear seemed to be that they would stress aspects of our history that were considered too liberal by some of the higher-ups. Since everyone worked from the same jointly planned course outlines at the special schools, it was unlikely that even an ardent Communist could have more than minimally affected any class.

All the faculty members complained about the barely adequate staffs. The plans for Eustis actually had to be altered because of the size of the staff. Lecture classes, originally scheduled to be taught four times daily to groups of five hundred, were reframed to accommodate twice as many men two times a day. But the crucial security clearance, which took time and which few passed, had to be met. Dr. Moulton commented that because of the tightness of the organization, personal views didn't have much effect on the courses. He added: "I couldn't care less. Suppose we had a few Communists? It wouldn't have affected anything."

The CID apparently suspected one of the German refugees, an "idea man" at SPD headquarters, of being a Communist and feared his influence on Colonel Davison. A few Germans had been selected to work with the program without much being known about them except that they had fled Hitler and were educationally qualified. Hitler's greatest enemies in Germany, of course, were Communists, so the CID fanatics were provided a convenient label for German refugees, true or false. The CID also suspected the high intellectual level of the Americans in the project. They never had much confidence in the leaders of the program, whom they described as being "too intellectual" and "too overenthusiastic" with "somewhat impractical ideas." The description was probably valid, but only the most narrow-minded of men would consider those characteristics undesirable.

Pressure was great by the time the Getty program began. It got worse as teachers became more and more difficult to obtain. But because they believed in each other and their work, spirits remained high among the faculty at the school—as this poem demonstrates:

> *I sing of Fort Getty, that school by the jetty,*
>   *Where prisoners come in by the score*
> *And are processed so quickly that, though they*
>   *come thickly*
>   *We always have room for one more.*
> *Among its chief features the absence of teachers*
>   *Is something the Army desires,*
> *Since re-screening students from motive of prudence*
>   *Is a task at which one never tires.*
>
> *I sing its T/O, so exceedingly low,*
>   *It has festered a school for police,*
> *Where a major named Kolster pulls from his holster*
>   *a course*
>   *Till Washington tells him to cease;*
> *But as part of our plan is to break every man*
>   *Who believes in the aim of the school,*
> *A distant autocracy wars with democracy—*
>   *And suspects are sent back to the pool.*
>
> *There's Dell and there's Behrendt, there's Ehrmann*
>   *(that parent!)*
>   *And Mommsen and Peters are there,*
> *There are Smiths in battalions, but not even*
>   *medallions*
>   *Of bodies who've faded to air!*
> *American history here is a mystery,*
>   *Since there's no one to teach it at all,*

And if any should know some, or possibly show some,
We plant him behind the eight ball.

We're doers, not planners, we're personnel scanners,
The catsup we have has turned blue
Lest someone be able to come to our table
And whisper "It's red—just like you!"
When we seek our abode, we walk straight down the
road,
We veer not, nor wander, nor diddle,
For we know we are pure and completely secure
So long as we stick to the middle.

To hell with God's-sakers! We're bottleneck breakers,
We complain not, nor grumble, nor howl,
And daily by phone our bread (turned to stone)
Is delivered on orders from Powell.
Our staff work completing, we then take a beating,
And pray every night to provide
The thirty-odd men that we asked for again
Before they have transferred or died.

If we're skillful in blarney, the boat goes to Kearney,
If not we remain where we are;
We have jeeps, and they're ducky, and O! if we're lucky,
Perhaps we can get there by car.
We admire Major Moore and we feel very sure
He is stuck in the middle like us,
But My God, if we could, how we would, how we would
Go over to Kearney and cuss!

How much damage the Red scare did to the reeducation
program is difficult to measure. It resulted in a desperate shortage of faculty for the Getty, Wetherill, and Eustis special

projects; the loss of the very valuable Howard Mumford Jones; the loss of McKnight, the dedicated and able deputy director (he was transferred to another branch after one fight too many over transfers by the CID); the decimation of the talented headquarters staff; the meddling into proved methods by uninformed outsiders; and the loss of a number of talented and skilled individuals from the four special schools who either quit in disgust or were removed by the CID. The Getty-Wetherill-Eustis projects held together only because a small group was dedicated to the job despite the army.

The Red-baiting also may have led to the rejection of many students from the Eustis and Wetherill projects. One very poignant letter exists from a half-Jew (who had gone from a concentration camp to the 999th Probationary Division) who was rejected from Wetherill. The reason, he believed, was because a friend of his in a POW camp had been an overt Communist. He could not believe he was not trustworthy enough to collaborate with the military government merely because of one friendship. He was not the only one in a similar situation. Were they Communists, or merely too liberal by CID standards, or guilty by association? There is no way to tell without seeing their screening tests, which no longer exist. In fact, alleged Communist leanings was the reason many were rejected from both schools. Were the POWs aware of the army's attitude toward Communists? The prisoner's letter above and others indicate that they were. They noted in letters to the War Department that this seemed odd in a democracy and inconsistent with what they had learned about the Bill of Rights. We did not always seem to practice what we preached. It was a bad way to teach American "values."

On someone's order, too, *The German-American* was occasionally banned from all camps "on the ground that it has Communist leanings." William L. Shirer and others protested this very strongly in February 1945, but the decision was made. Since the paper appeared sometimes and not others, the fact that it was being censored was painfully obvious. This policy could easily have made a mockery of freedom of speech and freedom of the press in the eyes of some of the POWs. After taking the time to set up a reeducation program, the army seemed determined to cause it to fail by hindering and contradicting it all along the way.

After V-E Day, many Nazi fanatics jumped on the Communist bandwagon in the camps to goad the Americans. At many camps, Nazis told American authorities that "Communism was the next 'Weltanschauung' and that Russia is the only salvation." Considering that Communists in Germany had been Hitler's archenemies, this phenomenon can more easily be explained by the fact that the prisoners were well aware of the army's phobia about the extreme left. Granted, the newspaper accounts of luxury in the Russian POW camps encouraged the Nazis, but the frantic reactions any hint of Communism got from the army must really have fired up the troublemakers.

Despite all the setbacks, a fair evaluation would never label the reeducation program as a failure. As has been shown, the polls proved there were some positive results in the prisoners' attitudes, and, as Dr. Moulton noted: "We didn't do anything catastrophically wrong, and we could have."

In a self-evaluation, the SPD likened its mission to a hastily constructed and manned Liberty ship armed to perform a vital but mysterious war task. Admittedly, the voyage was difficult at times. Right after V-E Day, "the entire crew was seized with violent seasickness and the vessel almost ran aground on a treacherous, unchartered reef—'Food Restriction Reef.' "

But through all blustery winds, typhoons, and adverse currents, the ship never strayed from its course. The SPD's self-evaluation recorded:

Finally, the ship neared its destination, somewhat battered and worn, but *there*. It was not surprising that the journey had been difficult. It was not important now that leaks and cracks developed, that certain members of the crew and even some of the mates, perhaps, had lacked the necessary judgment and experience. Even that a portion of the cargo had to be sacrificed could not detract from the fact that the mission was unexpectedly successful. Most important—it proved that *the trip was possible.* It blazed a trail and charted a course in the wake of which other vessels may and should follow.

SPD administrators and teachers were very realistic about their work. The one accomplishment of the program that they unanimously agreed had to be noted in an evaluation was that it did the Americans a lot of good. As Dr. Moulton commented: "This was, we felt, the most positive, constructive thing that was done. I've always felt that if I had to be in the war, at least I was teaching. It was a *con*structive thing to do in something as *de*structive as a war."

The polls indicate that the staff at least moved the majority of prisoners in the right direction from the American point of view. Each believed the program was a success. Kunzig adds: "First of all, it cost the government almost nothing. There were funds created by the expenditures by the prisoners in the canteens that paid for it. And many fine people went back to positions in Germany in the media, television, newspapers, politics. I'm sure it couldn't have done any harm, and it probably did a lot of good."

On one thing, the feeling of the staff was unanimous: if they were able to alter the attitude of one prisoner who ultimately affected a German policy decision, the program was a success. Each replied: "If one Walter Hallstein had in any way gained feelings toward the United States that were good feelings from being at Getty, it could be worth the entire program."

Did the Germans have to be entirely reoriented? Some might argue that all that was needed was for these men who had lived so long under Nazi oppression—learning, reading, and hearing only the twisted Nazi picture of the world—to have all the closed doors reopened. They could learn the truth about history, the arts, and much more in the American camps. Maybe that was true for some, but the comparison of Eustis men with the rest seems to indicate that, indeed, a lot of reeducation work was necessary. If anything, the Eustis-Shanks-Atlanta poll showed that to come close to completely eradicating the scars of the past, more than mere intellectual diversion was needed. What changed their minds were the things they learned in the classes about American life and tastes, about civics, geography, and history, about Jews, blacks, and other *verboten* people.

If one agrees that Nazism was by definition an evil philosophy that preached hatred, war, and genocide, then using the nonviolent means at one's disposal to end its reign was justified and, in fact, necessary. The SPD seized the opportunity and the means to do just that. They did not, and could not, forcibly attempt to brainwash. They strongly pointed out the evil of the Nazi system and offered a more attractive alternative on a voluntary study basis. They made the materials for self-improvement via democratization available, and many, if not all, rose to the challenge.

No one can accurately predict what any individual will ever do with his talents or with what he is taught. The SPD put together the best men and materials they could in a short time and, against adversity from all sides, including the War Department, did a remarkable job of turning the prisoners away from the learned responses of their past toward a new way of running their lives and country. If even a few were taught to use their native talents to work against ever seeing another Hitler in Germany, and consequently toward democracy as a system of government, then the program was certainly a success.

 # The War Is Over

SINCE THE WAR DEPARTMENT had intended the reeducation program to eventually be of help in the rehabilitation of Germany, the SPD hoped that things would be well planned for the returning students and that they would somehow play a role in a democratic West Germany.

To speed up the process, prisoners from Forts Kearney, Getty, and Wetherill were flown to Germany in small groups as soon as it was felt they were ready to pursue the roles for which they were trained. But those from Eustis went by ship, debarking at Le Havre, France.

Unfortunately, the army was not set up to implement its own program. Coordination was so disorganized at the port in New York that the former AEOs sent ahead to await the Eustis graduates in France had no idea which ships carried the select prisoners. They had to meet every incoming shipment of POWs and search for special groups from Eustis. The officers assigned to escort each group often could not get berths on the same ships as their charges. Some, luckily, got passage on speedier vessels than the Victory ships carrying the prisoners. Others arrived at Le Havre late, to find their specially trained hopefuls sitting in isolation confinement in the local stockade or at POW Camp Bolbec, the only places they could be quartered.

Thanks to the War Department and the French, the prisoners, who had been so diligently taught the glories of democratic life, got an instant education in the less glamorous and more disorganized side of life in a free society. As if ending up in the local stockade weren't bad enough, the prisoners discovered that not all democracies are as rich and as kind as America. The French had been none too generous with their prisoners. Camp Bolbec, where most of the Eustis men eventually stayed, and other holding camps in France were a nightmare compared to accommodations in the United States. Many barracks had dirt floors, no heat, no electricity, and limited running water.

The French, who had insisted on having all the returning Germans work on rebuilding projects, were so poorly organized that whatever reconstruction was being done was being planned and accomplished by the Germans themselves. German prisoners joked that the SS was again in control of Normandy.

Literally hundreds of thousands of Germans were crowded into POW camps in France. All the men captured in the last weeks of the war were housed along with those returning from the United States and other Allied nations. The situation was so chaotic that without their SPD escorts, who managed somehow to keep them separate so they could be rushed ahead to Germany, the special prisoners from Eustis who were supposed to help convert Germany would undoubtedly have ended up stuck in the confusion in France instead.

The tireless escorts saw that trains were provided to begin the trip home. However, the railroads were still subject to army regulations regarding troop and equipment movements, which meant that every forty miles the engine was detached and sent back down the line while the passengers waited for an engine to arrive from the train that was supposedly ahead of them. In

addition, the French railroad workers were not overly cooperative. Often, no engine or no train at all was ready, because the
French balked at moving any POWs out before reconstruction
was finished. Several escort officers reported how they goose-
stepped around, shouting commands with pistols half unhol-
stered, borrowing a technique from the former enemy to get the
Frenchmen moving.

Robert Kunzig accompanied one of the early Eustis groups
on the train trip to Germany. Their arrival in the fatherland was a
time of mixed emotions. As the train crossed into the Saar region
from France, the men crowded to the car door for a first glimpse
of home. What they saw, in stunned silence, was desolation and
destruction. Only mounds of rubble were visible where towns
once thrived. Even though forewarned, they had not expected it
to be so bad.

As the trains wound through villages and towns, they were
met at each station by hordes of people looking for relatives. They
brought ersatz coffee and bread. The prisoners shared their
chocolate and cigarettes from America. There was welcome chat-
ter while the endless questions about fathers and sons were
asked.

In Germany, troop movement was a bit easier. An SPD
officer had prepared the arrival points at Heilbronn and Bad
Aibling for the special shipments of men. Military discharges and
repatriation were expedited.

Specially prepared as they were, the prisoners from the four
select schools must still have been overwhelmed by the conditions in their homeland. Destruction from aerial bombing had
left towns and cities mere shells. Only one-third of the homes in
Frankfurt and less than half of Hamburg remained, and with
other cities and industrial centers in no better shape, housing was
in short supply.

The German Army had consumed most of the country's
dwindling supplies of necessary goods in the last months of the

war. There was little food, little fuel, inadequate clothing and medicine in most areas.

Many were sick from malnutrition or other diseases caused by deprivation. In Hamburg alone in late 1946, there were a hundred thousand people suffering from edemas due to under-nourishment. In Cologne, 90 percent of the children were below normal weight for their height and age. It was the same everywhere. To make matters worse, more than two million displaced persons left homeless and landless from the war or Nazi racial policies had arrived in Germany to be relocated.

Naturally, the occupation had brought its own problems to the already desperate country. Blackmarketeering, drunkenness, venereal disease, and illegitimate pregnancy flourished. In the American zone the latter two problems were particularly severe, partly because the strict antifraternization laws forced relationships to be covert. (The lifting of the fraternization ban improved the situation considerably in late 1946.)

A large number of the thirty thousand man from the four special schools in the United States did find jobs that aided the occupation government or the rebuilding of Germany. But the difficulties were numerous, and while some succeeded, others gave up.

Once they managed to find their families, then to decently house and feed them,* the special prisoners began appearing at military government offices, the German civil service, schools, newspapers, and universities looking for work. They faced two immediate obstacles.

Their first problem in getting military government jobs was that, despite a memo allegedly sent out to all manpower officers, few knew what the men were talking about. They carried small,

*Although all those selected for Getty and Wetherill were supposed to be from the Western zones, many had to move whole families out of the Russian zone when they arrived home.

easily forged diplomas signed by Alpheus Smith, an unknown name in the military government, saying they were graduates of a special school at Kearney, Getty, Wetherill, or Eustis. The attitude they met was: "Big deal." Those among the later batches of arrivals carrying papers as proof of their completion of a reeducation course at Fort Benning, Camp Concordia, or other regular camps had even less of a chance. At least the SPD sent around officers to explain what the four special schools had been. Due to that extra effort, many commanders did agree to at least consider placing a diploma-bearer on the staff, but many turned a deaf ear.

Kunzig spoke of the men he encountered: "It was very hard because a lot of them would have their own favorites. They wouldn't necessarily give a damn about this. People would say, 'What do I care if this guy went to some course in Rhode Island?' But if you struck a good man—and many of them were—he'd say it sounded like a good idea. So you'd give him the names of certain people. Then you'd tell them to see him. You were trying to see that it didn't die."

Many special prisoners did obtain jobs in the military government this way. Once they had proven themselves able, they brought their friends from the special projects into the office. Only in that indirect way did Getty or Eustis men get any special treatment.

But there was a second, greater stumbling block which affected the prisoners' abilities to get jobs in any of the positions vital to reeducation and democratization in Germany: the denazification laws of the occupation.

The denazification laws prohibited anyone who had been a member of any of the Nazi-affiliated groups or the Nazi Party from holding any elective office, teaching, or having any position of authority and responsibility. After a time the law was modified to punish only the most hard-core Fascists, but early in 1946 the special arrivals from the United States ran head-on into the purification restrictions. Theoretically, these were trained democrats, so there should have been no problem. However, this was not the case.

Denazification procedures at the projects had been limited. The screening was meant to turn up wolves in sheep's clothing— hard-core Nazis posing as democrats. Many men who had perhaps joined party organizations to save their jobs but were not Nazi believers were allowed into the schools. In prewar Germany, membership in Nazi-affiliated groups had been required in order to keep a job in some professions. Embarrassing as it seemed to them later, many joined so they could work. Still others had joined the party out of patriotism in the first years of the Nazi reign but had regretted it once Hitler had revealed his genocidal and war aims. The tests at the projects were not meant to stop men in those two categories from entering. All those accepted for the schools had proved in tests to be good anti-Nazi-minded people. But some could never pass the occupation test because they fit into those borderline groups.

One of the reasons the SPD had not fought harder for guaranteed positions for graduates in Germany was precisely the denazification problem. Dr. Moulton explained: "If we had sent them over with a slip of paper saying, 'Hire this man for the military government,' and then one couldn't pass the denazification test, it would have queered the whole business."

In fact, to the knowledge of the SPD, two Getty graduates failed the test. In one case a former teacher was found to have joined the Nazi Party in 1938. His Getty identification papers were taken away by the military government, and he was not allowed to teach in occupied Germany. In the other case, another former teacher moved to Italy to find suitable work after being rejected for his brief party membership.

Although immediate postwar locating of former prisoners and their jobs was not easy, the SPD did keep up with a number of men. Dr. Moulton recalled that when he went to Germany to investigate the whereabouts of a cross section of special prisoners in the winter of 1946-47, fraternization and food restrictions of the occupation were still in force. Americans were not supposed to enter German homes or eat or drink in German restaurants, while Germans were not allowed in American areas. Moulton had to choose neutral locations, like park benches, as rendezvous spots.

Almost 20 percent of the Kearney and Getty graduates stayed in contact with their instructors in the United States for several years after repatriation. Nearly all of them occupied positions of responsibility and usefulness. The largest group of special trainees, of course, was from Fort Eustis. Unfortunately, only about 15 percent of these men were traced. Considering the quick training they had received, the SPD was very pleased with the work they found.

In March 1946, Colonel Davison wrote to Alpheus Smith that there was "ever-increasing evidence to show that the prisoners trained at the Rhode Island installations . . . are making a most valuable contribution to the conduct of civil affairs" in Germany.

Military government work was the immediate answer in employment for some of them. Four Getty graduates assisted the military government in Karlsruhe, Baden-Württemberg. One was a legal assistant and a military court prosecutor at Rothenburg, Bavaria. Two worked for counterintelligence. In Berlin a Getty graduate worked in the food and agriculture branch.

Through a former Eustis friend, John Hasslacher received a clerical job with the Export/Import Agency of the military government in Munich. He immigrated to the United States in 1949 and now resides in Colorado.

The attitude of the German government, the *Länder* (state) governments, the universities, and other institutions was more open to the special arrivals. Although denazification provisions restricted employment here, too, the more intelligent and progressive leadership in the new Germany welcomed these men. The director of the state employment and labor service of Baden-Württemberg directed his assistants to hire any Eustis graduate who applied. "These men understand conditions better than most people," he told Kunzig. "They aren't dreaming of a dead past; they're building for a decent future."

Many Getty and Kearney men found employment in German administration in a variety of important capacities. Two were advisers to the state economic ministries—in Hesse and Bavaria. One became an interpreter for the state government in Munich, and one an aide to the minister-president of Baden-Württemberg. Still others were employed by the ministry of culture in Stuttgart and by the national Council of States.

Of the Wetherill graduates, only five were personally traceable. The most important of them became the police commissioner of Kassel. (He was also the only one who could be found doing police work in Germany.) Two worked for the military government doing screening for the army's German employment office in Berlin. One found a post in the German civil service.

Several Eustis men received jobs that should have gone to Wetherill graduates. Upon arrival at Bad Aibling, they were grabbed by authorities for the Frankfurt police force. Two Eustis graduates became active in politics in the Russian zone. One was actually called back to the United States. His skill in languages and willingness to accept low pay earned him rapid immigration status to act as an interpreter for the army.

A number of Eustis men got good jobs in their state civil services. One worked on youth activities in Wiesbaden; another was an interpreter in the Karlsruhe administrative court.

In the field of education, a Getty man was responsible for textbook coordination and the rebuilding of schools in the Kultministerium of Stuttgart (the Kultministerium would be equivalent to a local Department of Health, Education, and Welfare in the United States—it's hard to think of a more perfect spot for a career in reeducation). Another taught at the University of Tübingen in the French zone. Two taught foreign languages at schools in Stuttgart and Karlsruhe, while another taught advertising in Hamburg (British zone). One principaled a secondary school, while six taught at that level.

Dr. Walter Hallstein became rector of the University of Frankfurt and quickly jumped into high government positions which led to his ultimate involvement in the Common Market. However, Hallstein says his Getty schooling did not help him as much as his prewar associations. But, he added, he made many friends in the camp, "and they are still my friends today."

Naturally, the physicians among them, much in demand, found positions in disease control and in hospitals without delay. One, in fact, was in charge of venereal-disease control in Mannheim.

In the media, where Kearney men in particular could be useful to the reeducation plans of the occupation, they readily found jobs.

Curt Vinz's first job was as culture editor of the *Wiesbaden Courier*. Later, he opened his Munich book-publishing house, Nyphenburger Verlagschanlung; at the same time, he and two other Kearney men published the newspaper *Der Ruf* for a few years, continuing the work they had started in the United States.

Two Kearneyites got into radio work. With the help of some smooth talking by a special projects officer, one became educational director of Radio Frankfurt, and the other a director at Radio Stuttgart.

Others excelled in the field of journalism. Several wrote for the *Wiesbaden Courier*, and two, an artist and a correspondent, worked for the *Neue Zeitung* of Munich. The *Stuttgarten Zeitung* and the magazine *Sie* were edited by Kearney and Getty graduates, respectively.

Eight men from Eustis who were traceable, and probably many others from the special projects and the more successful camp schools, returned to college. Although this kept them out of active roles in occupied Germany, their presence surely must have provided some impetus toward progressive curricula at universities.

Three societies were established—in Munich, Wiesbaden, and Stuttgart—by Kearney and Getty graduates for all holders of special-projects diplomas. In 1947 the Demokratische Gesellschaft in Munich also included prisoners not involved in the special projects in its membership of four hundred. At monthly meetings, prominent persons from various fields would speak and lead discussions, usually on immediate German problems. The Munich group also gave assistance to members and nonmembers alike (especially newly returned POWs) in obtaining clothing, shelter, legal assistance, and other services.

In Stuttgart, twenty former prisoners founded the Staatsburger Gesellschaft. At two conferences organized by the club, notables from the public and private sectors discussed urgent problems—particularly the housing and fuel shortages in the coming winter. More than five hundred ex-POWs attended the meetings.

The group also sponsored round-table discussions on Radio Stuttgart, lectured to school assemblies, held public forums, and developed a plan for adult education via radio. One former Gettyite, then an official in the Stuttgart ministry of culture, arranged for the ministry to sponsor a special school under the auspices of the Stuttgart group. Opened at Schloss Coburg, near the town of Schwäbisch Hall, the school was patterned after the program at Getty. It was a training ground for teaching citizenship in democracy to returning young former soldiers.

Dr. Hallstein helped establish the American Institute at the University of Frankfurt. Educators hoped in 1947 that the institute would sponsor the same kind of activities as the Stuttgart society and foster international relations and understanding.

Despite the rather neutral, sometimes unpleasant reception the special prisoners received from their fellow Germans, who sometimes regarded them with suspicion as collaborators, these groups gained ground. It became quite fashionable for a while to have been a Getty or Eustis man. Many falsely claimed they were in order to gain prestige or jobs.

In Austria, the People's Party and the Socialist Land organization both ran summer schools to train younger members for leadership in their respective parties. Both groups sought prisoners trained at the special schools in the United States to do the teaching. Three were found immediately; they were local government officials in the state of Salzburg.* In the summer of 1946, the entire class at the Austrian police school at Strobel and some of the faculty were POW graduates of the special American reeducation schools.

The work of all the specially trained ex-prisoners was undoubtedly helpful to war-weary Germans, who now found they had to adapt to a new way of life. The Munich, Stuttgart, and Wiesbaden groups helped their neighbors in many ways—by assisting them in locating housing and filling other immediate needs and by organizing some forms of education so they could begin to gradually absorb a new sociopolitical outlook. The work they did coordinated nicely, too, with the reeducation work being done by the Allies.

In all three Western zones, reeducation of the entire German populace was the master plan. The United States and Britain, particularly, put great emphasis on reeducation. For this they received considerable criticism from the Germans, who by the end of 1946 felt they were being unjustly victimized.

In the American zone, the army established information centers, libraries, and cultural clubs in thirty towns. The occupation philosophy was that a healthy democracy would spring from the political development of the individual. To that end, youth

---

*Actually, it was not that easy for the returnees to work in Austria. The Austrian civil service gave them fourth priority after members of the anti-Nazi underground, those imprisoned by the Nazis, and those dismissed from jobs by the Nazis. Eustis graduates were theoretically excused from loyalty examinations, but delays in the arrival of records from the United States often held up employment for weeks.

groups, children's villages, student welfare work by private groups, and student hostels were all encouraged. American films were made readily available, the army having learned (possibly in the American POW camps) the value films could have. German newspapers published by totally apolitical, non-party-affiliated sources were supported.

Central to the American idea of democratic reorientation was the rapid return to elections. By the end of 1946, the program to establish a degree of local and state self-government based on free elections and political responsibility had progressed significantly. Village elections were held in January of that year. Rural districts and town districts voted in April and May. The populace voted in state assembly elections in November and December.

In the British zone, some cultural centers were established, and British publications of all types were easily accessible. But the British mixed too much into internal politics, Konrad Adenauer, the late chancellor of West Germany, wrote in his memoirs. They handed newspaper publication over to the political parties and tried to swing the control of local politics to the Social Democrats (the Labour Party was, by then, in charge in England). Yet their attempts at reestablishing local institutions and governments in many places, like Cologne, were successful.

Many argued that the French had the best reeducation program, because it was the least overt. The French program was called "free learning" instead of reeducation. They had a much broader and more varied film program than the other zones. They established schools for teachers, programs at the University of Mainz, rewrote textbooks, and introduced the French baccalaureate exams. Student exchange between French and German universities were encouraged on a much wider scale than in the American or British zones. But the Germans never saw a French newspaper or magazine. This was indicative of the main failing of the French program: the isolation of the zone and its programs from those of the other Allies. For example, a union leader in the French zone could not meet with his counterparts in other zones. Coordination, unification for the future, and national goals for a new beginning suffered as a result.

In all three zones, German theater was quickly reestablished, but with an international flavor. Works by Thornton Wilder and Jean Anouilh played to packed houses. More foreign works were demanded and received.

Try as they might, however, the Allies could not succeed in winning real enthusiasm for any type of government or political life in Germany. Apathy and fear resulting from East-West tensions (divided Germany was right in the middle), ambiguities in governmental responsibility, boredom with the fact that it was the old Weimar people who had taken the lead politically, and residual Nazi influence made it clear that Allied plans were too ambitious and incomplete. Obviously, democracy would not be attained until the normal conditions of life could prevail and thereby provide the Germans with the opportunity to do the necessary work from within.

Perhaps the most significant effect the returning prisoners had in this regard came not so much from the special prisoners who had attended the four schools as it did from the prisoners as a whole. It would appear from surveys taken in 1946 and 1947 that the SPD had indeed taught a large number of the prisoners a great deal which they put into practice after the war.

Groups of former prisoners from camps all over the United States and other Germans were tested by the Office of Information Control (OIC) of the military government in Baden-Württemberg, and the military government in Berlin tested former Getty prisoners. The surveys showed that a high percentage of all POWs returning from the United States were more realistically concerned about the problems of rebuilding and selecting a form of government than other Germans.

These prisoners showed more insight into current problems resulting from the Hitler dictatorship and the war and had a more favorable attitude toward the necessity for reorientation from the

Nazi experience than most Germans. The groups tested by the OIC were 87.3 percent actively or passively interested in politics, while more than half of the rest of the population disclaimed any interest at all. There was no significant difference between responses of the average former prisoner and the Gettyites in this area of the poll.

The prisoners were also more liberal than the general populace. Sixty percent supported the Social Democratic Party, while only 27 percent of their countrymen in the American zone did. Only 10 percent of the reeducated prisoners backed the Christian Democrats (compared with 40 percent of the local citizenry).

Comments from all the returnees indicated that they were disillusioned with the German administration and believed it would be a long, difficult road to a democratic Germany. Nearly two-thirds felt that the German people were not yet ready to accept democracy and to live by its principles. They complained about the continued stranglehold of bureaucracy and the depth to which Nazi influence had penetrated the people. They were far stronger in support of a thorough denazification program than the population as a whole.

The impression of the OIC surveyers was that the POWs had returned from the United States very impressed with America, politically alert, and acutely aware of the problems of their country and its future. They hoped Germany could attain the individual growth, standard of living, and urbanism of the United States. They were, however, in danger of becoming disillusioned by the hard, unsympathetic environment in which their fellow-citizens approached their problems from an individualistic rather than a social viewpoint.

The only appreciable difference between the general POW groups from the United States and the Getty group was that the Gettyites showed a greater willingness to run for political office and had actually joined political parties (35 percent joined the Social Democrats, and 3 percent the Communists).

Of one thing the SPD could be sure, in retrospect: a majority of the prisoners they had tried to reeducate were sufficiently convinced about democracy to work hard for it in Germany. They ran for office, worked on political campaigns, and voted. Perhaps more important, they were not apathetic, as their countrymen were; caring, they followed politics, voiced opinions, and supported reeducation work—a sign that their teachers in America had succeeded as well as anyone could have hoped.

Of course, reeducation had to go far and deeply into the German way of life. There was no miracle cure that three hundred thousand or so ex-prisoners could effectuate, no matter how well reeducated. In 1956, the year the democratic constitution became law in West Germany, 14 percent of the population were still professed Nazis. In repeated polls from 1949 to 1958, proportions of 7 to 15 percent said they still liked Hitler, Goebbels, and the Nazi race doctrines, and that they blamed foreign powers for starting World War II.

A number of differently worded surveys throughout the 1950s repeatedly found 30 to 40 percent of the respondents to be anti-Semitic. As late as 1959, Jewish cemeteries were vandalized in Cologne. In 1953, 55 percent denied there had been any war crimes by the German military. But in the 1960s the effect of efforts by educators and others began to make itself seen. Only 15 percent wanted a mild sentence for Adolf Eichmann. Right-wing strength began to erode, and blame for the war began shifting to Hitler.

During the 1950s one-fourth of the German public unfalteringly condemned Hitler and opted for democracy in every poll. Obviously, they were not all returned prisoners from America, although one would assume the POWs were surely among them. It took a lot of work by dedicated Germans who did not forget what Nazism had really been to change the minds of the rest. They succeeded. By 1959 a democratic multiparty system was endorsed by 77 percent of the population. By the 1970s West Germany had become one of the wealthiest democracies in the world, and especially in the European Economic Community (Common Market).

The democratically inclined minority in West Germany began to work in 1947 and created a truly German self-reeducation plan to accomplish the task.

In Bavaria, the Academy for Political Education was established in 1956. It trained schoolteachers, adult educationists, civil servants, and those in public life in democratic principles. It also arranged conferences among those doing the reeducating and conducted social research. It was similar in design to the groups established by returning special prisoners ten years before.

At the Technical University in Berlin, a method of liberal arts study called *Studium generale* was developed as a reeducation device. By 1956 it was compulsory for all students to spend one semester at humanistic studies. This meant that for the first time in the history of German higher education, students would not be studying *only* in their area of specialization. They would have to take political science, economics, history, sociology, and other social sciences and humanities courses. For once, Germany's young adults would be able to make intelligent, informed decisions when confronted with political ideology or slogans.

Perhaps the most important development was the establishment of chairs in political science at major universities. At the Free University of Berlin alone, seven chairs were established (at the Hochschule für Politik). An Institute for Political Science was founded. These were "firsts" in a country that had always been educationally minded. It had never occurred to German educators that politics was a subject for study until the postwar era. Perhaps if such classes had been offered in the 1920s, Hitler's brand of politics might have been seen for what it was before it was too late.

Two institutes for political study—in Munich and Berlin— were formed to carry out an important role in adult reeducation. Study centered around political theory, political institutions, international relations, economics, and sociology. The Munich school provided lecturers for Bavarian teachers colleges and was responsible for an important series of political publications.

Democratically organized student associations also grew on campuses, and some of the leaders were former POWs. Other methods of increasing interest in government were tried. School groups observed the Bundestag and state assemblies in action. The federal government established an information service which produced a weekly paper, *Das Parlament* ("Parliament"), reporting on debates. Everywhere the Germans themselves were doing their best to educate people to the value of having a democratic system.

It was inevitable that, once freed of Nazi oppression and disdain, German church leaders would begin a drive to reestablish Christian principles and churchgoing in the nation. Protestant leaders met in Stuttgart in 1945, within weeks of V-E Day, and founded an evangelical academy for reeducation. By 1954 it had seven branches, with more than twenty thousand students at the Hannover school alone.

The West German Basic Law (*Grundgesetz*, or constitution) was a triumph for the most democratic forces in the country. In contrast to other constitutions, which place civil liberties in the preamble or amendments, the Basic Law, approved in 1956 by the Bundestag, puts the protection of civil liberties in the constitutional text itself—at the very beginning. The first paragraph of Article I proclaims that the dignity of the individual must not be threatened.

The third paragraph lists basic rights that all executive and judicial authorities are bound to defend. These include freedom in writing and painting; outlawing of sterilization or medical experiments (even with volunteers); equal rights for men and women; nondiscrimination in regard to sex, descent, race, language, religious or political views.

Article IV guarantees freedom of religion and conscience, the free profession of religious or philosophic views, and the right to refuse to serve in the military for reasons of conscience. Article

V protects freedom of opinion, research, and teaching. Article VI protects marriage and the family. Other articles guarantee the right of assembly and the right to join and found organizations.

Clearly, it is drawn heavily from the Bill of Rights and American civil liberties, with additional, anti-Nazi-inspired guarantees.

The Basic Law also adopted the principle of the American Constitution by which the powers of the federal government are expressed and enumerated while those of the *Länder* (states) are residual. But it also borrowed from the Swiss in building its definition of federalism with the heavy intermingling of federal and state governments in their direct effect on the people. The state administrations serve as executors of federal law in many cases.

One cannot help but remember the negative predictions of hundreds of writers, including famous sociologists and such respected columnists as Max Lerner (who wrote in 1945 that "The Chances Are Dark for a Democratic Germany").

Despite the blundering, heavy-handed reeducation effort of the occupation, and despite the residual effects of Nazi rule, a pro-American, democratic system did succeed in West Germany. It is the achievement of many dedicated Germans who remembered the fear and horror of living under Hitler. Many of those received their inspiration and training in prisoner-of-war camps in the United States. They may have tipped the scales; they may merely have added a few more voices to an inevitable movement. But they were there; they helped.

NOTES

Notes

ALL REFERENCES to events or incidents at particular camps, unless otherwise cited, were found in either the alphabetical camp records or the incident reports, both contained in ARCH 1 and ARCH 2. Publication information for books and articles which is not included here may be found in sources consulted. (More detailed references will gladly be furnished to future researchers on request.)

Introduction

Page

p.1   Total number of prisoners held by the Allies is an estimate based on figures in the Modern Military Branch of the National Archives, Washington, D.C. No final certified count of war prisoners was ever made.

p.1   Number of prisoners in the U.S.: Lewis and Mehwa, *History of Prisoner of War Utilization by the United States Army*, page 91.

p.2   Eleanor Roosevelt data: from interview by author with Maxwell S. McKnight, March 25, 1975.

p.2   Treaty of Prussia: Fooks, *Prisoners of War*.

p.4   McKnight: This and all subsequent quotes from Mr. McKnight, unless otherwise cited, are from two interviews between McKnight and author held March 25, 1975 and Oct. 27, 1975.

p.4   Number of prisoners: Lewis and Mewha, *op. cit.*

1

Page

p.7   Helmut W.: This and all subsequent quotes from Helmut W. are from his diary which was found in ARCH 1.

p.7   Numbers of prisoners: Lewis and Mewha, *op. cit.*

p.8   Interrogation and Intelligence information comes from ARCH 6.

p.10   Italians as stowaways: ARCH 2.

p.10   Richard S.: This and all subsequent quotes from Richard S. come from his diary found in ARCH 1.

p.11   Halting shipment of Italian captives: Lewis and Mewha, *op. cit.*

p.12   Number of prisoners: *ibid.*

p.14   Property complaints: from ARCH 8.

p.14   Field officer: Earl M. told this to Paul Wiesenfeld in 1969.

p.15   Interrogation and Intelligence: ARCH 6.

p.15   Shirer: from ARCH 5.

p.16   Interrogation complaints: ARCH 8.

p.17   Criteria for allowing prisoners to join Allied units: from ARCH 2.

p.18   Butner: This and all subsequent quotes about Camp Butner come from "An Informal History of the Re-education Program at Camp Butner" found in ARCH 1 and ARCH 2.

p.18   Letter to Grand Duchess: from ARCH 2.

p.19   Polls of prisoners: from WNRC 1.

p.19   SS tattoos: memo from Gen. Edward Witsell in ARCH 2.

p.19   Malmédy: from ARCH 2.

p.20   Letter from Lauretta N. Smith to author July 21, 1975.

2

p.23   Crossville: *Time*, "Behind The Wire," June 21, 1943.

p.23   McAlester: *The Daily Oklahoman*, "Prisoner of War Camp," Nov. 14, 1943.

p.23   Shelby: This and all subsequent references to Camp Shelby, unless otherwise cited, come from "History of Camp Shelby" in ARCH 2.

p.25   Concordia: This and all subsequent references pertaining to Camp Concordia, unless otherwise cited, were found in "A History of Camp Concordia" in WNRC 3.

p.26   Shoes: John Janes, "PW," *Family Circle*, May 5, 1944.

Page
p.27   Josef K.: This and all subsequent quotes from Josef K. were
            gathered in an interview he granted to Lori Palomone in Germany,
            July 1975.
p.28   Schools: Swiss Legation Circular No. 14 in ARCH 2.
p.30   POW mail: Archer L. Lerch, "The Army Reports on POWs," *The
            American Mercury*, May 1945.
p.32   Willie V.: This and all subsequent quotes from Willie V. were found
            in an intelligence memo dated June 12, 1944 in ARCH 2.
p.33   Employment contracts: Lewis and Mewha, *op. cit.*
p.33   Profit: Archer L. Lerch, "Handling German Prisoners in the United
            States," *Prisoner of War Bulletin*, Vol. 3, No. 5.
p.34   Fort Devens: Bernard Peterson, "What's Behind the American
            Salute by German Prisoners at Fort Devens," *Industry*, April 1945.
p.34   Man-day totals: Lerch, "Handling German Prisoners in the United
            States," *op. cit.*
p.35   Gene W.'s ranch: "PWs at Work," *The Daily Oklahoman*, Nov. 28,
            1943.
p.35   Ron D.: interview with author March 19, 1976.
p.35   Whittington: transcript of phone conversation, ARCH 2.
p.36   Union problems: Lewis and Mewha, *op. cit.*
p.37   Truman: *ibid.*
p.37   Bryan: *Report of Committee on Military Affairs*, 79th Congress, H.
            Res. 20, 1945.
p.38   Hitler: taken from William L. Shirer, *The Rise and Fall of The Third
            Reich* who quotes Felix Gilbert, *Hitler Directs His War*, Oxford
            University Press, New York, 1950, p. 179.
p.38   Coddling study: *Report of Committee on Military Affairs*, 78th
            Congress, H. Res. 30, 1944.
p.39   Orb: *Newsweek*, "Anger at Nazi Atrocities is Rising but United
            States Treats Prisoners Fairly," May 7, 1945.
p.39   Congressman: *The New York Times*, April 23, 1945.
p.39   Hartt: *The New York Mirror*, March 14, 1945.
p.39   Pampering: selected magazine articles and "On Pampering Prison-
            ers," *Collier's*, August 12, 1944.
p.40   Hasslacher: letter to author January 26, 1976.
p.40   Post V-E Day: from *Eighth Service Command Communique*, May
            4, 1945, No. 4, in ARCH 2.

3

p.42   Information related to the McKnight quote: from John D. Millett,
            *The Organization and Role of the Army Service Forces, United
            States Army in World War II: The Army Service Forces.*

Page

p.43   Fort Douglas: *Time*, July 23, 1945.

p.44   McAlester: ARCH 8.

p.44   Hoover: J. Edgar Hoover, "Enemies at Large," *American*, April 1944.

p.45   AWOL escape: ARCH 8.

p.45   Chicagoans: *Chicago Tribune*, May 28, 1945.

p.45-46   Papago Park escape: ARCH 2 and many newspaper and magazine articles.

p.46   Wattenberg data: *Time*, Jan. 8, 1945.

p.46   Lerch: press conference Feb. 13, 1945 in ARCH 2.

p.49-51   Ludwig W.: from appropriate camp records ARCH 1.

p.51   Karl P.: *ibid*.

p.52   Gottfried S.: based on Vicki Baum, "Land of the Free," *Collier's*, August 19, 1944.

p.52-53   Sentences: from ARCH 2, ARCH 8, and Richard Whittingham, *Martial Justice*, Chicago, 1971.

p.56   Camp Chaffee: from ARCH 8.

p.56   Camp Wheeler: Pat Patterson, *The Saturday Evening Post*, April 21, 1945.

p.57   Chandler, Arizona: *Atlanta Constitution*, April 10, 1945 and other publications.

p.59   James H. Powers, "What To Do With German Prisoners—The American Solution," *The Atlantic Monthly*, Nov. 1944, pp. 46-50.

p.59   S. L. A. Marshall: This and all subsequent quotes from General Marshall were contained in a letter he wrote to the author May 18, 1975.

p.62   Start of reeducation program: OCMH Manuscript 4-4.1, BA 1.

4

p.65   Richards: letter to author June 14, 1975.

p.66   Jesting evaluation: from "Hysterical Monograph" in Beinecke.

p.67   Original program outline: Beinecke.

p.67   Van Etten and Kearney start: OCMH manuscript 4-4.1, BA 1.

p.67   Kunzig: This and all subsequent quotes from Robert L. Kunzig, unless otherwise cited, were gathered in interviews with author March 18, 1975 and Oct. 1, 1975.

p.70   Hocke: found in ARCH 1, ARCH 2, ARCH 5 and in letter from Dr. Hocke to author June 23, 1975.

p.70-71   Operations at "Factory": OCMH manuscript 4-4.1, BA 1.

p.71   *Der Ruf: ibid*.

Page
p.73   SPD joked: "Hysterical Monograph," Beinecke.
p.73   *Der Ruf*: March 6 edition found in ARCH 2.
p.75   *Der Ruf* comments: "What They Say About *Der Ruf*," *ibid*.
p.75   Vinz: This and all subsequent quotes from Curt Vinz were contained
           in his letter to author April 17, 1975.
p.77   Camp papers and *Die Auslese*: OCMH manuscript 4-4.1, BA 1.
p.77   *Children in the U.S.A.*: in ARCH 2.
p.78   Bermann-Fischer: copyright memo in ARCH 1 and quote from
           Bedroht-Bewahrt (Frankfurt/Main, 1967), page 241, was contained
           in the Vinz letter to author.
p.80-81   Film: OCMH manuscript 4-4.1, BA 1.
p.82   Englander tease: "Hysterical Monograph," Beinecke.
p.84   T. V. Smith, "Behind the Barbed Wire," *The Saturday Review of
           Literature*, May 4, 1946.
p.84   Jones: in ARCH 2.
p.85   Lerch letter: Sept. 11, 1945, in ARCH 2.
p.85   McKnight: letter July 1945, copy in McKnight personal papers.
p.86   AEO data: OCMH manuscript 4-4.1, BA 1.
p.86   Speakman quote: unpublished Master's Thesis of Cumins E. Speak-
           man found in OCMH.
p.87   Anti-Semitism: ARCH 1 and ARCH 2.
p.88   Quotes: from original program plan at Beinecke.

5

p.89   State Department memo: ARCH 1.
p.90   Division goals: from original program at Beinecke.
p.90   Christmas gifts: ARCH 2.
p.90   Banned authors: ARCH 1.
p.91   Canteens: ARCH 2.
p.95   Davison: "Observations on Strategy," ARCH 1.
p.96   Respect for colleges: from original program at Beinecke.
p.96   Civilians: OCMH manuscript 4-4.1, BA 1.
p.97   Fort Bragg: "Report on School Activities POW Camp School, Fort
           Bragg, N.C.," in ARCH 1.
p.98   Heinreid C. at Ft. Bragg: ARCH 1.
p.98   Horst B.: "Poll of German Prisoner of War Opinion," ARCH 1.
p.99   Hans T.: unsolicited letter in ARCH 1.
p.99-100   Promote films: OCMH manuscript 4-4.1, BA 1 and ARCH 1.
p.101   AEO quote: Speakman thesis, *op. cit*.
p.102   Film catalogue: ARCH 1.

Page
p.102   McAlester: *The Daily Oklahoman*, Nov. 14, 1943.

p.103   Concentration camp booklet: ARCH 1, ARCH 5, and others.

p.104   *Times*: memo from Davison in ARCH 1.

p.106   *Chicago Tribune*: Transcripts of phone calls in ARCH 1.

p.108   Fort Devens: ARCH 1.

p.108   Fort Dix: *Time*, May 1, 1944.

p.109   Trinidad: ARCH 2.

p.109   Exhibits: directives in ARCH 1 and ARCH 2.

p.110   Book contest: suggested press releases in ARCH 1.

p.110   Ernst D. undated letter; Claus Von W. letter, Dec. 18, 1944; and Erich F. undated letter: all in ARCH 1.

p.111   Religion: from Camp Butner information ARCH 1.

p.112   Camp Mackall: ARCH 1.

p.112-113 SPD reaction: "Hysterical Monograph," Beinecke.

p.113   Seger: memos 8/1/44, 7/27/44, 7/14/44, and newspaper clips in ARCH 2.

p.114   Shirer: "Start Reeducation on Prisoners," *Washington Post*, Dec. 1944, "Writes William L. Shirer in the N.Y. Herald Tribune," *Reader's Digest*, Jan. 1945.

p.114   Harless: *The New York Times*, April 23, 1945.

p.115   Russians: Henry C. Cassidy, *The Atlantic Monthly*, Nov. 1944.

p.116   Waco: *Waco News Tribune*, Jan. 31, 1945 and transcript of telephone conversation in ARCH 1 and memo ARCH 1.

p.116   Letters from Florence and Indianola: ARCH 1.

p.116   Declassification memos in ARCH 1.

p.116   Canadians: lectures of Dr. George W. Brown, University of Toronto, in ARCH 1.

p.117   Bryan: memo May 29, 1945 in ARCH 1.

p.117   *Collier's*: June 2, 1945.

p.117   *American* magazine: Beverly Smith, July 1945.

p.118   *Wille und Weg*: in ARCH 1 and ARCH 2.

6

p.121   History of project: OCMH manuscript 4-4.1, BB1 C1.

p.121   Totals: *ibid*.

p.121   Tests: "Evaluation of Tests administered to Special German Prisoners of War," in ARCH 1.

p.121   U.S. Zone: memo March 14, 1945 in ARCH 5.

p.122   Percent: "Evaluation of Tests . . ." in ARCH 1.

p.122   Moulton: This and all subsequent quotes from Dr. Moulton were gathered at an interview with the author July 23, 1975.

Page
p. 123   Kunzig: letter July 25, 1945 in Beinecke.

p. 123   Hallstein: This and all subsequent quotes from Dr. Hallstein were contained in his letter to author Dec. 15, 1975.

p. 124   Dieter Zander: *New York Herald Tribune* Forum, Oct. 30, 1945. Broadcast over WOR and Mutual Broadcasting System 9:45 to 10:00 P.M. EST. Copy of speech from Moulton personal papers.

p. 124-125 Hallstein commencement address: Class No. 2, Oct. 20, 1945, from Moulton personal papers. (Delivered in English.)

p. 125   Status conscious: Henry Ehrmann, "Experiment in Political Education," *Social Research*, Sept. 1947.

p. 125   Alpheus Smith: letter from Lauretta N. Smith to author, August 25, 1975.

p. 126   Texts: OCMH manuscript 4-4.1 BB2 C1.

p. 126-127 Content of classes: *ibid.*

p. 127-128 Howard Mumford Jones: *The New York Times Book Review*, August 5, 1945.

p. 128   Content of classes: OCMH manuscript 4-4.1 BB2 C1.

p. 129   T. V. Smith, "Behind the Barbed Wire," *op. cit.*

p. 129   Requests at Getty: Kunzig and Moulton personal interviews as already cited.

p. 130-131 Language program: William G. Moulton, "Our Profession in Reverse," *The Modern Language Journal*, Oct. 1948.

p. 131-132 Experts: Case # 3871, POW Screening project in ARCH 1.

p. 132   Lie detector: *ibid.*

p. 132   Rejects: many letters in Wetherill Files in ARCH 1 and ARCH 2.

p. 133   Wetherill Curricula: outline in McKnight personal papers.

p. 133   Graduates: OCMH manuscript 4-4.1 BB2 C1.

p. 134   Teaching: Moulton, "Our Profession in Reverse," *op. cit.*

p. 134   Henry Smith: from Moulton interview as cited.

p. 135   Psychiatrist's report: letter from Dr. Brickner to Alpheus Smith in ARCH 1.

p. 136   Committee Psychological report: "Study of German PWs," (Liberty Project), Dec. 1945 in ARCH 1.

p. 137   Jones: Commencement Class No. 1, Sept. 8, 1945 from Moulton personal papers.

7

p. 141   Quota: memo Dec. 11, 1945 in ARCH 1.

p. 141   Screening: *ibid.*

p. 141   White, gray, and black: OCMH manuscript 4-4.1 BB1 C1 and "Consolidated Cycle Report" in ARCH 1.

Page

p. 142   Investigation in Germany: Quentin Reynolds, "Experiment in Democracy," *Collier's*, May 25, 1946.

p. 142   Total men: OCMH manuscript 4-4.1 BB1 C1 and ARCH 1.

p. 142-143   Reynolds: All quotes credited to Quentin Reynolds in this chapter can be found in "Experiment in Democracy," *Collier's*, May 25, 1946.

p. 143   Prisoner possessions: memo Dec. 11, 1945 in ARCH 1.

p. 143   Smith speech: OCMH manuscript 4-4.1 BB1 C1.

p. 144   Casady: Edwin Casady, "The Reorientation Program for PWs at Fort Eustis," *The American Oxonian*, July 1947.

p. 144   Personal problems: OCMH manuscript 4-4.1 BB1 C1 and Casady, *ibid*.

p. 145   Entrance pool: Casady, *ibid*.

p. 145   Course content: This and all other references to specific course material, unless otherwise cited, came from "The Six-Day Cycle," class outlines in ARCH 1.

p. 146   Wilhelm T.: This and all other POW reaction to classes or films at Fort Eustis, unless otherwise cited, came from "A Reorientation Program Seen through the Eyes of German Prisoners" in the Moulton personal papers.

p. 146   Second POW quote: from "Poll of German Prisoner of War Opinion" in ARCH 1.

p. 147-148   Evenings: OCMH manuscript 4-4.1 BB1 C1 and "A Reorientation Program Seen through the Eyes of German Prisoners" as cited.

p. 149   Wilfried S.: "Poll of German Prisoner of War Opinion" in ARCH 1.

p. 151   Course material: Henry Ehrmann, "Experiment in Political Education," *op. cit.* and "The Six-Day Cycle" as cited.

p. 152   Casady: Casady, *op. cit.*

p. 153   Exit pool: OCMH manuscript 4-4.1 BB1 C1 and *ibid*.

p. 154   Alpheus Smith quote: Reynolds, "Experiment in Democracy," *op. cit.*

p. 154   Questionnaires: OCMH manuscript 4-4.1 BB1 C1 and memos in ARCH 1 and "A Reorientation Program Seen through the Eyes of German Prisoners," *op. cit.*

p. 155-156   Food and song: Moulton interview July 23, 1975.

p. 156   Prisoner comments: memo Jan. 29, 1946 Ehrmann to Smith in ARCH 1.

p. 156   Prisoner comments: undated letter in ARCH 1.

p. 156   Commencement Address: Moulton personal papers.

p. 157   Polls: memos in ARCH 1 and "Reorientation Program Seen through the Eyes of German Prisoners," *op. cit.*

p. 158   Hasslacher: letter to author Jan. 26, 1976.

p. 158-159   Alpheus Smith: quoted by Reynolds, *op. cit.*

p. 159   Escort officer: Report No. 2 on Special Prisoners in ARCH 1.

Page
p.159   Press Sortie: William White, "German Prisoner Pledges New Life,"
         The New York Times, March 7, 1946.
p.160   *Der Ruf*: OCMH manuscript 4-4.1 BA 1.
p.160   Henry Smith: from Moulton interview July 23, 1975.

8

p.161   SPD jested: "Hysterical Monograph," Beinecke.
p.163   Sociologists: Curt Bondy, "Observation and Reeducation of German
         POWs," *Harvard Educational Review*, Jan. 1944; H. L.
         Ansbacher, "Attitudes of German Prisoners of War: A Study of the
         Dynamics of National Socialistic Followership," *Psychological
         Monographs*, Vol 62, No. 1, 1948; Helen Peak, "Some Psychologi-
         cal Problems in the Reeducation of Germany," *Journal of Social
         Issues*, Aug. 1946; David M. Levy, "The German Anti-Nazi: A Case
         Study," *American Journal of Orthopsychiatry*, July 1946; and Hen-
         ry Ehrmann, *op. cit.*
p.163   Bondy, *op. cit.*
p.164-165 Eustis-Shanks-Atlanta Poll: "Poll of German Prisoner of War Opin-
         ion, Office of the Provost Marshal General" in ARCH 1 and ARCH
         2.
p.166   Sociologists: Ansbacher, *op. cit.* and Bondy, *op. cit.*
p.166   Quote from "What About the German Prisoner?," War Department
         pamphlet issued Nov. 1944 found in ARCH 1 and ARCH 5.
p.167   Trinidad: letters from John Hasslacher, Jan. 9, 1976, and Rudolf
         Werner, March 8, 1976, to author.
p.168-170 AEO evaluation of program: "Evaluation of Re-education Pro-
         gram—Section C" in ARCH 1.
p.170   Secretary of War: letter from Acting Secretary of War Robert P.
         Patterson, March 26, 1945 to Secretary of State in ARCH 1.
p.171   Lerch, *Der Ruf*, etc.: protest letter from Lt. J. Schevill, acting chief
         of the programs branch to Gen. Lerch, July 19, 1946, in ARCH 1;
         letter from McKnight to Davison, July 19, 1946, copy in McKnight
         personal papers.
p.171-172 Security checks: ARCH 4 Investigation Programs and Personnel
         Branch.
p.172   Loyalty checks: memo April 2, 1945 from Lt. W. Homiller to Davi-
         son, order of loyalty check attached to memo and signed by Lt. Col.
         A. Papa. In ARCH 4 Personnel Branch.
p.172-173 McKnight letter to Davison, July 19, 1945, copy in McKnight per-
         sonal papers.
p.173-174 McKnight letter July 21, 1945, copy in McKnight personal papers.

Page
p.174   Howard Mumford Jones: from Beinecke and McKnight interview with author Oct. 27, 1975.
p.174   McKnight: Transcript of phone conversation McKnight to Major Gemmill July 19, 1945. McKnight personal papers.
p.175   CID attitude: from 1975 interview with person who wishes not to be identified.
p.176-177 Poem: from McKnight personal papers.
p.178   Siegfried C.: letter Oct. 12, 1945 in Fort Wetherill file ARCH 1.
p.178   *The German-American*: memo to Generals Bryan and Lerch from Davison, Feb. 6, 1945 in ARCH 1.
p.179   Communism: memo July 28, 1945 in ARCH 5.
p.179-180 Evaluation: "Evaluation of Re-education Program—Section C," *op. cit.*
p.180   Hallstein: from already cited interviews with Kunzig, McKnight, and Moulton.

9

p.182   AEO Coordination: Report No. 2 on Special Prisoners in ARCH 1.
p.183   French camps: letter from D. Meyer to Hugo Mueller in ARCH 1.
p.183-184 Railroads and AEO story: letter from Lt. R. Mellman to Alpheus Smith in ARCH 1.
p.184   Kunzig: Robert L. Kunzig, "360,000 PWs—The Hope of Germany," *American*, Nov. 1946.
p.184-185 In Germany: Alfred Grosser, *The Colossus Again*; John Gimbel, *The American Occupation of Germany*.
p.185   Occupation problems: Lucius Clay, *Decision in Germany*; Gabriel Almond, ed., *The Struggle for Democracy in Germany*.
p.187   Getty men: letter from Curt Vinz to McKnight, March 3, 1946 in ARCH 1.
p.188   Davison letter in ARCH 1.
p.189   Kunzig: *op. cit.*
p.189-190 All data on employment of POWs comes from the following:
         (a) memo to Office of Military Government for Germany (U.S.) from Dr. Moulton, June 26, 1947, Moulton Personal papers.
         (b) letters to Edwin Casady from former POWs 1946-48, Casady personal papers.
         (c) Kunzig, *op. cit.*.
         (d) letter to Gen. Bryan from PMG in Europe, Feb. 12, 1946, ARCH 1.
         (e) Job application for R.K. in ARCH 2.

Page

(f) letter from Curt Vinz to author April 27, 1975.

(g) letter from John Hasslacher to author Jan. 26, 1976.

(h) letter from Dr. Walter Hallstein to author Dec. 15, 1975 (including quote).

p.191 Societies and American Institute: memo to Office of Military Government (U.S.) from Dr. Moulton, *op. cit.* and Kunzig, *op. cit.*

p.192 Austria: memo July 26, 1946 in ARCH 1.

p.192 Police School: taken from picture information, U.S. Army Audiovisual Agency, Pentagon, Washington, D.C.

p.192-194 Reeducation in Germany: Clay, *op. cit.*; Grosser, *op. cit.*; Gimbel, *op. cit.*; Almond, *op. cit.*; Richard Hiscocks, *Democracy in Western Germany*; and Alfred Grosser, *The Federal Republic of Germany*.

p.194-195 Surveys: "U.S. Training Held Help to Germans," *The New York Times*, Feb. 16, 1948 and "A Reorientation Program Seen Through the Eyes of German POWs," Moulton personal papers.

p.196 Statistics in Germany: Roy Macridis and Robert Ward, *Modern Political Systems: Europe*.

p.197-198 Reeducation within Germany: Hiscocks, *op. cit.*

p.198-199 Basic Law: Macridis and Ward, *op. cit.* and Robert Neumann, *The Government of the German Federal Republic*.

p.199 Lerner, "The Chances Are Dark for a Democratic Germany," *PM*, March 26, 1945.

SOURCES CONSULTED

INDEX

Sources Consulted

FROM THE NATIONAL ARCHIVES, MODERN MILITARY BRANCH:

RG 389 (PMG) Prisoner of War Special Projects Division, Administrative Branch, Decimal File, 1943-46, Boxes 1593-1655. (Cited as ARCH 1 in footnotes)

RG 389 (PMG) Enemy Prisoner of War Information Bureau Reporting Branch, Subject File, 1942-46, Boxes 2468-2714. (Cited as ARCH 2)

RG 389 (PMG) Prisoner of War Operations Division, Legal Branch, Numeric Subject File, Boxes 1513-24, and Operations Branch, Unclassified Decimal File, Boxes 1310-12, and Information Bureau, Subject File, Boxes 1581-82. (Cited as ARCH 3)

RG 389 (PMG) Internal Security Division, Coordination Branch, Subject File, 1937-46, Investigative Program, Boxes 1846-48, 1828-32; and M.G.P. 49 (PSD Activities), Boxes 1892, 1894; and Subversive Program, Boxes 1909-14, 1917, 1928-29, 1879-80; and Postwar Planning, Box 1915; Security Intelligence Corps and School, Box 1925; and Personnel Box 1913. (Cited as ARCH 4)

RG 407 Army Adjutant General Classified Decimal File, 1943-45, Decimal 383.6, Boxes 2437-51. (Cited as ARCH 5)

RG 165 Chiefs of Staff, (G-2) Intelligence Division, Captured Personnel and Materials Branch, Enemy POW Interrogation File (MIS-Y) (W.D. General Staff) Boxes 359 and 361. (Cited as ARCH 6)

FROM THE NATIONAL ARCHIVES, OPERATIONS AND POLICY DIVISION:

Decimal 383.6: Box 1299, Cases 28, 33, 38, 80, 134; and Box 1302, Case 185. (Cited as ARCH 7)

FROM THE NATIONAL ARCHIVES, STATE DEPARTMENT BRANCH:
RG 59 Department of State Records, 1942-44, World War II—German Prisoners of War, File Number 711.62114. (Cited as ARCH 8)

FROM THE WASHINGTON NATIONAL RECORDS CENTER, MODERN MILITARY BRANCH:
RG 208 Office of War Information, NC-148, Entry 407, Boxes 2191-92. (Cited as WNRC 1)
RG 208 Policy Subject File, Office of Policy Coordination, Office of Director of Overseas Operations, Office of War Information, Box 116, Entry 359. (Cited as WNRC 2)
RG 338 Army Commands, United States, 1942, Military Review, Command and General Staff College, Fort Leavenworth, Kansas, History of POW. (Cited as WNRC 3)

FROM THE OFFICE OF THE CHIEF OF MILITARY HISTORY:
Records at the OCMH consist of War Department Special Staff Historical Division Manuscripts which are cited in the footnotes as OCMH with the manuscript number. I looked at the eleven manuscripts which related to POW education although the entire list of manuscripts related to World War II is several pages long.
Also on file at OCMH were the following:
Speakman, Cumins E., "Re-education of German Prisoners of War in the United States During World War II," unpublished Master's Thesis, University of Virginia, 1948.
Provost Marshal General's Office: "Office of the Provost Marshal General, A Brief History," Pt III: "Prisoners of War." Unpublished monograph, Historical MSS, Department of the Army, 1946.

CONGRESSIONAL DOCUMENTS:
United States Congress, House, *Report of Committee on Military Affairs*, 78th Congress, H. Res. 30, 1944.
United States Congress, House, *Report of Committee on Military Affairs*, 79th Congress, H. Res. 20, 1945.
United States Congress, House, *The Congressional Record*, "Congressman Andrew J. May's Extension of Remarks," 79th Congress, 1st Session, March 5, 1945.

PRIVATE COLLECTIONS:
Edward Davison's Papers: on file at the Beinecke Rare Book and Manuscript Library, Yale University, New Haven, Conn. (Cited in footnotes as Beinecke)

INTERVIEWS:
Judge Robert L. Kunzig interviewed by author March 18, 1975 and October 1, 1975, in Washington, D.C.

Maxwell S. McKnight interviewed by author March 25, 1975 and October 27, 1975, in Washington, D.C.

Dr. William G. Moulton interviewed by author July 23, 1975 in Princeton, New Jersey.

Sid Richman interviewed by author May 1, 1975 in Chevy Chase, Maryland.

Ron D. interviewed by author March 19, 1976 in Silver Spring, Maryland.

Josef K. interviewed by Lori Palomone July 1975 in West Germany.

Earl M. interviewed by Paul Wiesenfeld in 1969 in northern Virginia.

LETTERS:

From Dr. Walter Hallstein to author December 15, 1975.

From John Hasslacher to author January 9, 1976 and January 26, 1976.

From Dr. Gustav René Hocke to author June 23, 1975.

From Brigadier General S. L. A. Marshall to author May 18, 1975.

From Robert F. Richards to author June 14, 1975.

From Lauretta N. Smith to author July 16, 1975 and August 25, 1975.

From Curt Vinz to author April 27, 1975.

From Rudolf Werner to author March 8, 1976.

PERSONAL PAPERS:

Edwin Casady's personal papers and letters from 1945-48 re: Forts Getty and Eustis and POWs returned to Germany.

Maxwell S. McKnight's personal papers and letters from 1943-46 re: reeducation, Red scare, POWSPD organization.

Dr. William G. Moulton's personal papers re: Fort Getty language program, Fort Eustis, and returned POWs.

BOOKS:

Adenauer, Konrad, *Memoirs, 1945-53*, Henry Regnery Company, Chicago, 1966.

Almond, Gabriel A., ed., *The Struggle for Democracy in Germany*, University of North Carolina Press, Chapel Hill, 1949.

Brickner, Dr. Richard M., *Is Germany Incurable?*, J. B. Lippincott Co., New York, 1943.

Clay, Lucius D., *Decision in Germany*, Doubleday & Co., Inc., Garden City, New York, 1950.

Flory, William S., *Prisoners of War: A Study in the Development of International Law*, American Council on Public Affairs, Washington, 1942.

Fooks, Herbert C., *Prisoners of War*, Federalsburg, Maryland, 1924.

Gimbel, John, *The American Occupation of Germany*, Stanford University Press, 1968.

Grosser, Alfred, *The Colossus Again*, Frederick A. Praeger, Inc., New York, 1955.

——, *The Federal Republic of Germany*, Frederick A. Praeger, Inc., New York, 1964.

Hiscocks, Richard, *Democracy in Western Germany*, Oxford University Press, London, 1957.

Jaworski, Leon, *After Fifteen Years*, Gulf Publishing Company, Houston, Texas, 1961.

Lewis, George and Mewha, John, *History of Prisoner of War Utilization by the United States Army: 1776-1945*, Pamphlet No. 20-213, Washington, Department of the Army, June, 1955.

Macridis, Roy C. and Ward, Robert E., *Modern Political Systems: Europe*, Prentice-Hall, Inc., Englewood Cliffs, N.J., 1963.

Millett, John D., *The Organization and Role of the Army Service Forces, United States Army in World War II: The Army Service Forces*, Office of the Chief of Military History, Washington, Department of the Army, 1954.

Neumann, Robert G., *The Government of the German Federal Republic*, Harper & Row, New York, 1966.

Pabel, Reinhold, *Enemies Are Human*, The John C. Winston Company, Philadelphia, 1955.

Shirer, William L., *The Rise and Fall of the Third Reich*, Simon & Schuster, Inc., New York, 1959, 1960.

Whittingham, Richard, *Martial Justice*, Henry Regnery Company, Chicago, 1971.

MAGAZINES, PERIODICALS, AND JOURNALS:

"Anger at Nazi Atrocities Is Rising but United States Treats Prisoners Fairly," *Newsweek*, May 7, 1945, p. 58.

Ansbacher, H. L., "Attitudes of German Prisoners of War: A Study of the Dynamics of National-Socialistic Followership," *Psychological Monographs* Vol. 62, No. 62, No. 1, 1948, pp. 1-41.

"Axis Prisoners in the United States," *Prisoner of War Bulletin*, American Red Cross, Vol 1, No. 2., p. 9.

Baum, Vicki, "Land of the Free," *Collier's*, Aug. 9, 1944, pp. 11 ff.

"Behind the Wire," *Time*, June 21, 1943, pp. 67.

Bondy, Curt, "Observation and Re-education of German POWs," *Harvard Educational Review*, XIV, Jan. 1944, pp. 12-17.

"Boss of 200,000 Enemies," *American*, May 1944, p. 131.

Brown, John Mason, "German Prisoners of War in the United States," *American Journal of International Law*, XXXIX, April 1945, pp. 198-215.

Casady, Edwin, "The Reorientation Program for PWs at Fort Eustis, Virginia," *The American Oxonian*, July 1947, pp. 146-54.

Cassidy, Henry C., "What To Do With German Prisoners—The Russian Solution," *The Atlantic Monthly*, Nov. 1944, pp. 43 ff.

Cook, F. G. Alletson, "Democratic ABCs for Nazi POWs," *The New York Times Magazine*, Nov. 11, 1945, pp. 8 ff.

——— "Nazi Prisoners are Prisoners Still," *The New York Times Magazine*, Nov. 21, 1943, pp. 12 ff.

"Death and Treason," *Newsweek*, Feb. 5, 1945, pp. 47-48.

Devore, Robert, "Our 'Pampered' War Prisoners," *Collier's*, Oct. 14, 1944, pp. 14 ff.

"Do We Pamper POWs?," *Collier's*, June 2, 1945, p. 75.

Ehrmann, Henry W., "An Experiment in Political Education," *Social Research*, Sept. 1947, pp. 304-20.

"Escape in Arizona," *Time*, Jan. 8, 1945, p. 16.

Hirsh, Diana, "German Atrocities Raise Questions: Are Nazi POWs 'Coddled' Here?," *Newsweek*, May 7, 1945, pp. 60-61.

Hoover, J. Edgar, "Enemies at Large," *American*, April 1944, pp. 17 ff.

Janes, John E., "PW," *The Family Circle*, May 5, 1944, pp. 20 ff.

Jones, Howard Mumford, "Writers and American Values," *The New York Times Book Review*, August 5, 1945.

Kunzig, Robert Lowe, "360,000 PWs—The Hope of Germany," *American*, Nov. 1946, pp. 23 ff.

Lerch, Archer L., "Handling German Prisoners in the United States," *Prisoner of War Bulletin*, American Red Cross, Vol 3., No. 5, pp. 4 ff.

———, "The Army Reports on POWs," *The American Mercury*, May 1945, pp. 536-46.

Lerner, Max, "The Chances Are Dark for a Democratic Germany," *PM*, March 26, 1945.

Levy, David M., "The German Anti-Nazi: A Case Study," *American Journal of Orthopsychiatry*, XVI, July 1946, pp. 507-15.

"Midnight Massacre," *Time*, July 23, 1945, p. 24.

Moulton, William G., "Our Profession in Reverse," *The Modern Language Journal*, Vol XXXII, No. 6, Oct. 1948, pp. 421-30.

"Nazi Prisoners are Nazis Still," *The New York Times Magazine*, Nov. 12, 1943, p. 38.

"Nazis in the United States," *Time*, May 1, 1944, p. 64.

"On Pampering Prisoners," *Collier's*, Aug. 12, 1944, p. 12.

"Our Growing Prison Camps: How U.S. Treats War Captives," *U.S. News and World Report*, May 28, 1943, pp. 23 ff.

Pabel, Reinhold, "It's Easy to Bluff Americans," *Collier's*, May 16, 1953, pp. 20 ff.

Patterson, Pat, "Handle with Gloves," *The Saturday Evening Post*, April 21, 1945.

Peak, Helen, "Some Psychological Problems in the Re-education of Germany," *Journal of Social Issues*, II, Aug. 1946, pp. 26-38.

Peter, Marc, "Prisoners of War and the International Red Cross Committee," *Prisoner of War Bulletin*, American Red Cross, Vol. 2, No. 3.

Peterson, Bernard, "What's Behind the American Salute by German Prisoners at Fort Devens," *Industry*, April 1945, pp. 7 ff.

Powers, James H., "What To Do With German Prisoners—The American Solution," *The Atlantic Monthly*, Nov. 1944, pp. 46-50.

"POW's Outbound," *Newsweek*, May 25, 1946, p. 34.

Reynolds, Quentin, "Experiment in Democracy," *Collier's*, May 25, 1946.
Smith, Beverly, "Nazi Supermen Hit the Dirt," *American*, July 1945, pp. 45 ff.
———, "The Afrika Korps Comes to America," *American*, August 1943, pp. 28 ff.
Smith, T. V., "Behind the Barbed Wire," *The Saturday Review of Literature*, May 4, 1946, pp. 5 ff.
"Swastika over Arizona," *Newsweek*, Feb. 26, 1945, p. 58.
"The Captive Enemy," *Newsweek*, March 29, 1943, pp. 33-34.
"The Kriegsmarine Escape," *Newsweek*, Jan. 8, 1945, pp. 33-34.
"The Masquerader," *Time*, March 23, 1953, p. 25.
"The Nation—Enough Nazis," *Newsweek*, May 21, 1945.
"Writes William L. Shirer in the N.Y. Herald Tribune," *Reader's Digest*, Jan. 1945, p. 44.

ARTICLES FROM BOOKS:
Casady, Edwin, "The Basic Assumptions of Democracy as Presented to German Prisoners of War," *Conflicts of Power in Modern Culture*, Lyman Hall, ed., published by Conference on Science, Philosophy and Religion, Harper & Brothers, New York, 1947.

NEWSPAPERS, A REPRESENTATIVE SAMPLING:
Atlanta Constitution:
Hartt, John, "Arizona's Tombstone Days Echoed As POWs Flashed Towel Swastika," April 10, 1945.
———, "Desert Town Protests 'Coddling' Nazi Prisoners," March 12, 1945.
Jones, Ralph, "Are We Too Gentle With War Prisoners?," March 26, 1945.
Bremer County Independent and Waverly Republican:
"War Prisoners Here Eat Bread and Water," Sept. 6, 1944.
The Boston Daily Globe:
"Only 6 of 25 Nazis Who Fled Camp Taken," Dec. 26, 1944.
Chicago Tribune:
"Aid War Prisoner," May 28, 1946.
"Army Thanks Tribune for Aid in Teaching Nazis Democracy," Sept. 11, 1945.
The Daily Oklahoman:
Moore, Morris P., "Prisoner of War Camp," Nov. 14, 1943, p. 14C.
Power, Del, "PWs at Work," Nov. 28, 1943, p. 14C.
The New York Mirror:
Hartt, Julian, "Finds 'Luxury' At Prison Camp Mostly a Myth," March 14, 1945.
The New York Times published regular stories from Jan. 1, 1943 to August 1, 1947. A selection are as follows:
White, William S., "German Prisoner Pledges New Life," March 7, 1946.
"Captives Schooled in U.S. Helping to Run Germany," April 25, 1946.
"Captives Trained to Police Germany," Sept. 23, 1945.
"180 German War Prisoners Sail," Oct. 29, 1945.
"Stimson Rejects Plan to Teach Nazi War Prisoners Democracy," Nov. 30, 1944.

"U.S. Training Held Help to Germans," Feb. 16, 1948.

The Washington Post. A selection are as follows:

Shirer, William L., "Start Reeducation on Prisoners," Dec. 1944.

"Nazi PWs Maintain Hope of Escape—But They Don't," Oct. 9, 1943, p. 8.

"Prisoner Problem," April 24, 1945.

"U.S. May Cancel Plan to Ship More Nazis Here," May 6, 1945.

Editorial, April 29, 1945.

IN ADDITION:

"Edward Davison, Poet and Teacher," *The New York Times*, Feb. 9, 1970.

"European Unity Architect: Walter Hallstein" (Man in the News), *The New York Times*, Nov. 18, 1966.

"Dr. Henry Smith, Jr., A Language Expert," *The New York Times*, Dec. 15, 1972.

Index

music, 31
  German military, 83
  in reeducation program, 28, 83,
    107-109
Music in America, 107, 143

National Catholic Welfare Council, 27
nationality problems, in repatriation,
    17-19
National Youth Administration (NYA)
    camps, 25
Nazi Party membership, postwar
    effect of, 187
Nazi POWs, 2, 6, 21, 75, 83, 136
  as anti-religious, 50, 110-111
  camp life dominated by, 40-62, 92
  Communism embraced by, 179
  conversions of, 165-167
  "courts of honor" of, 50, 51
  execution of, 52-53
  harassment of other POWs by, 41,
    47, 48, 49-55, 58, 60, 89, 90,
    93-94
  hard-core, percentages of, 47-48
  ideological suppression by, 48, 72,
    76, 81, 91, 104, 171
  killing of prisoners by, 52-53, 61
  medical care and, 54
  neutralization of, in reeducation
    program, 92-94, 99
  organization of, 48, 49-50, 51, 54,
    59-60, 92
  postal sabotage by, 54-55
  segregation of, 58-59, 76, 92, 94,
    98, 99, 122, 140, 141-142, 170
  suicide clubs of, 56-57
Nazism (*see also* Germany, Nazi), 40,
    43, 56, 92, 104, 162, 166, 181, 187
  in postwar Germany, 196
  atrocities of, 103-104, 148
Neue Volkszeitung, 113
Neue Welt books, 75, 78-79, 91, 110,
    143, 168
Neue Zeitung, 190
Neumaier, J. J., 150

Nevins, Allan, 128
newspapers, U.S., for POWs, 104-
    107
New York City, Nazi propaganda on,
    19-20
New York City Police, 133, 171
New York Herald Tribune, 15, 61
New York Staats-Zeitung, 104,
    105
New York Times, 60, 72, 104-105,
    106, 117, 159
North Africa, POW camps in, 8-12
novelists, POWs as, 109

Office of Information Control (OIC),
    194-195
Office of War Information (OWI), 77,
    79-80, 81, 102, 128, 150, 152
One World, 149
Orb, Camp (Germany), 39
Osborn, Frederick, 59, 65, 173n

Pabel, Reinhold, 12, 13, 14, 20-21, 23,
    29, 46
Paige, Dave, 59-60, 62, 96
Papago Park, Camp (Ariz.), 16, 39,
    45-46, 53, 57, 114
Peary, Camp (Va.), 155-156
Perry, Camp (Ohio), 72
Pima, Camp (Ariz.), 60
Pine Groves Furnace, Camp, 15
Plaunch, Camp (La.), 75
Pocket History of the United States,
    128
police training, 120, 121, 131, 133,
    136, 189
polygraph tests, 131-132
Pomona Ordinance Depot, Camp
    (Cal.), 45
posters, 94, 109-110
Power and the Land, 150
Powers, James H., 59
Prelude to Silence, 149
Preuss, Hugo, 126
Price, Arnold, 151